T0358204

# STOCKS
### and
# FOREX TRADING
## *HOW TO WIN*

# STOCKS
## and
# FOREX TRADING
### HOW TO WIN

**KAREN WONG • DARYL GUPPY**

 **World Scientific**

NEW JERSEY · LONDON · SINGAPORE · BEIJING · SHANGHAI · HONG KONG · TAIPEI · CHENNAI · TOKYO

*Published by*

World Scientific Publishing Co. Pte. Ltd.

5 Toh Tuck Link, Singapore 596224

*USA office:* 27 Warren Street, Suite 401-402, Hackensack, NJ 07601

*UK office:* 57 Shelton Street, Covent Garden, London WC2H 9HE

**Library of Congress Cataloging-in-Publication Data**

Names: Guppy, Daryl J., 1954–    author. | Wong, Karen (Certified financial technician), author.

Title: Stocks and forex trading : how to win / Karen Wong, Daryl Guppy.

Description: New Jersey : World Scientific, [2021]

Identifiers: LCCN 2021023184 | ISBN 9789811236860 (hardcover) |
    ISBN 9789811237645 (paperback) | ISBN 9789811236877 (ebook) |
    ISBN 9789811236884 (ebook other)

Subjects: LCSH: Foreign exchange. | Stocks.

Classification: LCC HG3821 .G86 2021 | DDC 332.64/2--dc23

LC record available at https://lccn.loc.gov/2021023184


**British Library Cataloguing-in-Publication Data**

A catalogue record for this book is available from the British Library.

For any available supplementary material, please visit
https://www.worldscientific.com/worldscibooks/10.1142/12274#t=suppl


Desk Editor: Lai Ann

Typeset by Stallion Press
Email: enquiries@stallionpress.com


Printed in Singapore

# Contents

# Acknowledgements

"Double Happiness plus One" was the title of the email starting it all. The email was to let Daryl know how happy I was. My 'double happiness' of having one of my trading concepts presented by him at the International Federation of Technical Analysts Annual Conference and the debut of my first published article in a trading magazine. The 'plus one' was an attempt at humour. Mentioning a dream goal, a book collaboration — Karen Wong and Daryl Guppy — I was half serious, but he was not. The outcome of this conversation is the book you're reading now.

Thank you to my husband Melvin, who in 2003 thought of trading as an ideal activity for me. He is my biggest supporter who encourages me to keep going even in times of my own doubt. Trading became a part-time job I could do from home while having my little boys by my side.

Little boys grow up. One little boy, who used to be my companion while trading, used his skills on a photographic shoot to produce my author photo. Daniel's contribution is greatly appreciated. The other little boy, now also fully grown, continues to accompany me. Thank you to the ever-patient Justin, who always makes time to listen to my trading concepts.

Daryl Guppy's first book *Share Trading* became the foundation of my knowledge on how to trade. Ten years after first reading it, we met at a conference and it was hard for anyone to understand my excitement. To me, meeting this walrus moustachioed person was like meeting a famous film celebrity — one of the best in his field. I was starstruck. Daryl asked me, "Do you trade?" My answer was, embarrassingly, "I trade on and off."

Starting a subscription to Daryl's newsletters — www.guppytraders. com — my trading eventually became more on than off. In an email to the editor, I mentioned finishing well in a national sharemarket game. Thank you to Ryan Guppy who first asked, "Would you like to write an article about that?" From this first article, I have continued to contribute newsletter articles about my trading experiences.

I cannot thank Daryl enough for encouraging me to become a better trader by learning through my experience of trading and finding the possible answers to my own questions. Daryl is generous with his time and is a pleasure to work with. He is a work colleague and also a friend. The man who wrote the first trading book I ever bought has now written a book with me.

Thank you to all my trading friends and other fellow traders I have met at conferences along the way. Your chats have often inspired writing topics for some of my articles. I hope this book helps you trade profitably into the future.

**Karen Wong**
Sydney 2021

# Introduction

I've always liked to play games. As a child, it was Hungry, Hungry Hippos then Cluedo and Monopoly. I've had a go at Call of Duty and Mario Kart, though failing miserably due to my lack of coordination and skills. Today I enjoy Animal Crossing: New Horizons and Splatoon on Nintendo Switch. Games have taught me to be a better problem solver as I am constantly thinking of strategies to win or to reach my goal. Playing for hours to win, to level up and sometimes to lose. Persistence was the key to improving as was learning from my mistakes.

The financial markets are similar to how games work — learn the rules, set up your strategies and play to win. For those starting out in the game of trading, a stock exchange market simulation game is an excellent place to start. Register and familiarise yourself with the workings of the market without risking a single cent.

In the past this was often sneeringly dismissed as monopoly or paper trading. That's no longer accurate as these games, just like today's Fortnite, are vastly more sophisticated and a far cry from Hungry, Hungry Hippos.

The best of the stock market simulation games is run by the Stock Exchanges and pit you against thousands of other traders rather than just a single brokerage client group. Playing this game honed my skills and confirmed my strategies, ranking me in the top 1.8% nationally out of nearly 18,000 players.

It was essential groundwork preparation for the real task of successful trading. What I learned in these games, and in developing strategies, saved me thousands of dollars in potential losses when I entered the market with real money. Used correctly, these games can do the same for you.

This is not just a book on theoretical trading. Real trade examples are used throughout to show you the interaction between the market and me as the trader. Through my personal trades I detail the decisions and the thinking behind each decision and the methods used to attain the best outcome for now or for next time. This gives you a better idea of what works, and which mistakes to avoid. We all make mistakes, buts it's the early recognition of mistakes that contributes most to successful trading.

When I first started trading, I was a young mother at home looking for income from part time work. Time was limited and the thought of trawling through pages of financial analysis was not appealing nor practical. Technical analysis was ideal for a time poor person like me. Using indicators to forecast price movements and to see the past performance of a stock laid out on charts was a shortcut way of seeing what was happening in the markets. Everything I needed to know or see was on a chart. The main indicator used in the charts of this book is the Guppy Multiple Moving Average (GMMA). A technical indicator developed by my co-author Daryl Guppy to determine direction, behaviour and character of a trend. This indicator works well combined with price action and other popular technical analysis patterns and indicators.

Once you develop a good strategy for one market, look at the possibilities of using it to trade in other markets. I prefer the GMMA as a foundation to trade the stock and Forex markets. The issues I faced and the methods found to be helpful when applied to trading Forex are explored in the later part of the book. Daryl Guppy takes you through the concepts of GMMA, Traders Average True Range (ATR) and the Average Daily Range (ADR). These are the components we consistently use in our trading. We hope to demonstrate how they work in different markets.

Trading is often seen as a way of making big money fast. It's also a way of losing big money. Fast. Focusing on the trade process and managing risk leads to successful trading. It's not only about the money. Chat with any trader and one of the main challenges is knowing exactly when to exit a trade at the best price. Banking in the maximum profit with minimum regret. Trading for over 17 years, I have had to make many decisions on many trades. Even with a clearly written trading plan, mistakes and losses are still inevitable as part of the trading game. Managing these risks are important to grow your profit and preserve capital. I'll share with you the ways I have managed risk on various trades from the decision-making process through to the outcomes.

My introduction to the world of technical analysis began with a book. It was written by my co-author Daryl Guppy whom I eventually met at a conference 10 years later in 2013.

Now it's time for Guppy to enter the introduction. After writing eight books the task of completing a jointly written book is a new exercise for me and entails one important decision. Should the authors speak with one voice, or with two distinct voices? In this book, we have chosen to speak with a blended voice so readers can focus on the content of each chapter rather than on the authorship.

As Karen noted, we first met at a traders' conference in 2013. Karen had written some articles for our weekly trading newsletter and I was impressed with her approach and writing. It's rare to find traders who can both trade and write clearly. Karen continued to submit articles to our newsletter and developed a substantial and impressive body of work. Just as importantly she brought different approaches to the market and different understandings.

The market I grew up with and where I learned my craft is not the market of today. The way I learned to approach and trade the market is no longer relevant. Karen is a much more recent participant. She brings with her the approaches more suited to today's generation of new traders and that's what makes this book particularly useful and relevant. Her work and insights deserved a broader audience and this book is the result. It is not a book I could write alone because I do not have this learning experience in this environment. This is very much Karen's book and I am pleased to have been able to offer assistance in this cooperative endeavour.

Post-GFC I worked on some new ways to understand, display and manage volatility as increased volatility had become a new and permanent feature of our markets. I turned my attention to Foreign Currency markets and developed approaches that met my requirements in terms of time and money management. The result was the ANTSYSS methodology. I spoke about this at conferences and refined the concepts and techniques, sharing them first with our newsletter readers. These are brought together for the first time in this book.

We divided the book into four sections. The first is STARTING WITH STOCKS. This section shows how the Stock Market Game run by a stock exchange formed a foundation of strategy and strategy testing that underpinned both trading stocks, and then later, trading derivatives and foreign currency. It is a modern approach for a social media aware generation.

WRESTLING WITH RISK is not a at length discussion of the 2% money management rule with pages of spreadsheet calculations. Instead, we focus on the risk challenges and methods displayed in price behaviour. It's a more practical discussion of when to hold the position and when to fold the position and when to run.

MIND MATTERS is a salutary section illustrating what happens when you let emotions take over trading decisions. These are the temptations that turn good profits into smaller profits and larger losses. This section gives you some examples of what you can expect to encounter. Hopefully, armed with foreknowledge, your reactions will be all the better.

The final section STEPPING UP TO FX considers what skills for the stock trader are required for successful trading in foreign currency markets. We look at the new skills needed and discuss the trading strategies most suited to the part-time independent trader. The construction and philosophy of the ANTSYSS trading methodology is included here. It's an approach designed to meet specific needs and is not intended as a general guide to trading FX markets.

Neither of us come from a background of working for a prestigious finance corporation and you do not have to either to be able to trade part time or full time successfully from your own home. We hope this book provides an inspirational source of ideas and methods. Establish your foundation or build on strategies you already use to achieve your trading success in a game known for being one of the hardest in the world to win. You won't win every time but played correctly good outcomes are possible.

**Karen Wong**   www.karenwong.net
**Daryl Guppy**   www.guppytraders.com
2021

# Part 1

# Starting with Stocks

# Chapter 1

# Ten Thousand Hours

Growing up in the sunny suburbs, I never dreamed of being an independent part-time trader but through my other work, I did develop the discipline required to make trading a success. It took me more than 10,000 hours to become a Certified Practicing Accountant and about 10,000 hours to become a qualified designer. Neither of these helped me to trade the market, although the discipline of learning served me well.

Trading is often seen as a way to get rich quickly. The call to abandon the grind of 9 to 5 and make a fortune from the comfort of your own home has beckoned many a wannabe trader. Trading for me was no sudden whim. It was a decision I made taking into consideration my personal circumstances of being confined to home at the time. I was looking for a way to earn an income after I saw my friends going out to work. Except, I wanted to do it all from home. I set out to teach myself so I bought a book and it all started from there.

The turning point of success followed a period of self-learning and the formal study of technical analysis, woven into multiple trade successes and trade failures that are part and parcel of the trader experience.

Over 10,000 hours of learning about how to be a good trader established my foundation for trading, enabling me to use technical analysis in order to succeed in the market. Ten thousand hours is approximately 417 days or three hours a day over nine years. It sounds daunting but there are ways to make this journey more efficient and profitable. This book provides a faster pathway. It's not as if you have to do all these hours before success arrives. I did over Ten thousand hours and worked in the accounting profession. With less than 10,000 hours I worked proficiently in the design industry. Ten thousand hours as a trader should be marked by success after success, profit after profit — and some inevitable losses — during the journey to professional mastery.

Perhaps you do not aspire to become a professional, but you need similar professional skills if you aspire to be a successful part-time trader. Just as you might aspire to be a good athlete, your aspirations don't necessarily mean your goal is to be selected to compete in the Olympics. However, aiming high improves performance and it's no different with trading.

Every profession requires many hours of practice and years of experience for an individual to become good at what they do. Traders are no exception when it comes to trading and trading well. Malcolm Gladwell, author of *Outliers*, writes, "It takes 10,000 hours of deliberate practice to become an expert". Gladwell counts only good practice. Defining good practice in trading means not only successful profitable trades. It includes acting on a stop loss for any trade not reaching its target profit. Most importantly it means acting on a stop loss to prevent a single losing trade from inflicting massive damage on your trading capital.

If I had my training time over again, this is where I would start with the first hour of those 10,000 — the stop loss. This is the armour protecting you when you take your first trade and go into battle with experienced professionals. I would love to say this is where I started but it would be false. I discovered this armour only after suffering several painful wounds, all eating away at my capital. It's up to you whether you armour-up first or wait until you feel the pain of crippling losses.

In this book, I start the journey with a losing trade example, not because I want to show you how to lose but because I want to show you how to survive, thrive, and win. Like most of the trades I discuss, this is a personal trade. These are not textbook examples. They are gathered from the many hours of trading required to make the book learning practical. The discussion gets technical because my trade methods are based on technical analysis. I briefly explain each indicator or method as it is encountered.

The following trade on Prime Media Group (PRT) demonstrates why it is best practice to act on a stop loss. As for all trades we need five pieces of information.

1.  **Trend direction** — This is the direction of where prices are heading. It is either going up, down, or sideways.

2. **Trend strength** — This is how strong or weak the trend is and whether it is likely to continue.
3. **Trade entry point** — The price you are prepared to buy at in order to position yourself for potential profit.
4. **Stop loss point** — The price you intend to sell at if you are wrong in order to limit your losses.
5. **Potential profit target** — The price you are happy to sell at to lock in your profits.

Figure 1.1 shows the Weekly chart of PRT. The long-term Guppy Multiple Moving Average (GMMA) and the short-term GMMA are marked. PRT was in a strong downtrend turned sideways until both the long-term and the short-term groups started to turn upwards. With the short-term GMMA group above the long-term GMMA group, the trend was up. This shows trend direction and trend strength.

The GMMA indicator was developed by Daryl Guppy and is available in many charting packages. It is used to understand the way investors and traders are thinking. The concept of the GMMA indicator is revealed as you read through the book.

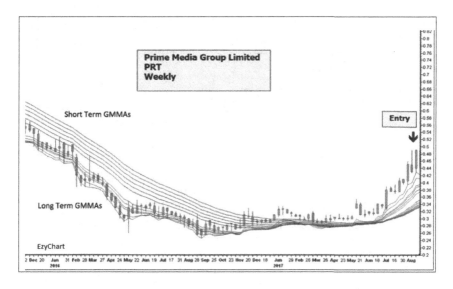

**Figure 1.1.** Weekly chart of PRT.

Flip forward to Chapter 23 if you need more detail but for the purpose of this example this is what you need to know. At the right side of the chart in Figure 1.1, the short-term GMMA shows the activity of the short-term traders. They are active in this stock. The long-term GMMA shows the activity of the long-term investors. Observing the degree of separation, the lines of the long-term GMMA show some strength in this uptrend. The Daily chart of PRT is where we search for an opportunity to enter a trade.

Figure 1.2 shows the Daily chart where we see the short-term GMMAs and the long-term GMMAs trending upwards. Both the short-term traders and the long-term investors were keen on this stock. The long-term GMMA shows well-separated moving average lines, confirming the strength of the underlying uptrend.

Next, we set the entry point and the stop loss point. We open a trade on PRT at the price of 0.45 and set an Average True Range (ATR) stop loss

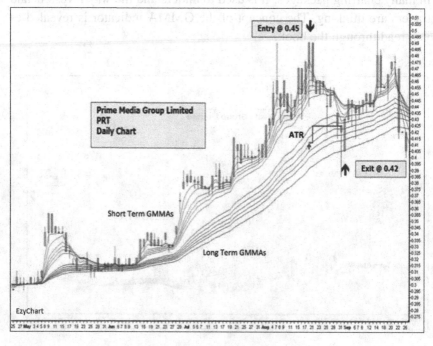

**Figure 1.2.**   Daily chart of PRT.

of 1. This is marked as ATR on the Daily chart by the single line drawn beneath the price action.

The Average True Range indicator was developed by Welles Wilder. It is a measure of price volatility. It shows how far, on average, we expect price to move as part of normal price behaviour. Any move larger than this may indicate a change in behaviour and a potential change in trend direction.

Placing the Traders ATR indicator on a chart is an essential part of my stop loss process. Flip forward to Chapter 24 if you need more detail but for the purpose of this example you just need to know this is the stop loss line. A move below this line suggests the trend direction has changed.

The ATR line shown in this chart is a Traders ATR and this application was also developed by Daryl Guppy. It is included in some charting packages. It takes the ATR value and displays it as a ratchetted value on the price chart instead of an indicator displayed underneath the chart.

An ATR stop loss of 0.41 is calculated and a Target Profit of 15% over the entry price is calculated at 0.52. In this example, the profit target is not really important. Survival is more important in this example. In future examples, we include the profit target because this is an essential part of calculating not how much money you could make, but the risk and reward ratio. This ratio determines your long-term success.

Our natural reaction when something hurts us is to turn away and close our eyes. Like many natural reactions, this does not serve us well in the market. The market gives us an opportunity to see our mistakes unfold. We analyse these, so the mistakes are not repeated in the future. An athlete watches a slow-motion replay of their sprint out of the blocks. Traders get to watch a day by day development of the price action after their trade is closed. It's often a slow-motion study in regret. There is much to be learned from these post-mortem trade developments.

On the following day, the price of PRT dropped and continued in a downward direction. The short-term GMMA had also turned down as short-term traders were selling the stock off. Price fell through and closed below the ATR stop loss of 0.42. I sold PRT the next day at the stop loss price of 0.42. This resulted in a loss of 6%. In retrospect it looked like we were entering the trade at the top of the chart and exiting the trade close to the bottom.

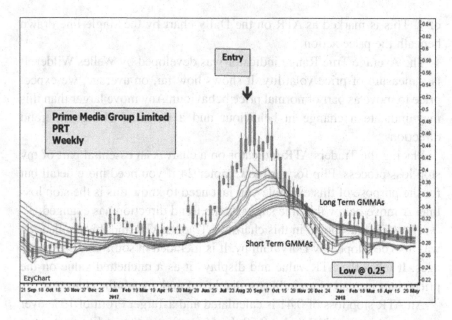

**Figure 1.3.**   GMMA exit conditions.

This is not fire and forget. Each loss, or victory, has lessons to teach. Following on after the trade was closed, we analyse the PRT chart as it develops in the days to follow to see what happened and if there are any lessons to take into our next trade.

Getting out was the right thing to do. On the Weekly chart in Figure 1.3, we see the short-term GMMA has compressed, turned over, and fallen through the long-term GMMA. Compression signalled agreement between the short-term traders on the price and value of PRT. It was an area of price weakness forewarning a possible change in direction and it became a prophecy fulfilled. A change in the trend occurred from an uptrend to a definite downtrend.

Price was at its lowest point at 0.25 on the Weekly chart. If we had ignored the stop loss, we could have been sitting on a loss of 44%.

Would you sell at 0.25? The answer is probably no. Many people — the unsuccessful investors and washed-out traders — hold on in the hope price would rise again to 0.45. If it does rise, then they make a promise to themselves to definitely sell at break-even. At break-even they wish for price to rise even higher so they actually make a profit. This is one of the great market fairy tales and it doesn't matter how many times they wish and kiss, this toad remains forever a toad and not a prince.

Better to avoid letting a small loss turn into an ugly toad. This example shows why it is essential to limit losses and preserve capital when a stop loss is triggered. If we need 10,000 hours of good practice to become good at trading then we need to include amongst other things, not only profitable trading but also the repeated discipline of acting on our stop losses.

This is the first hour in my 10,000-hour journey, restructured with the benefit of hindsight. The second group of hours is putting together your trading plan.

# Chapter 2

# Battle Planning

Prior to undertaking hazardous bombing missions over occupied Europe, B17 crews were given many hours of training. Trading is only a danger to your wealth rather than your health but unless we spend many hours practicing we won't develop the necessary skills to thrive in our chosen vocation. When you aspire to become a trader you want to do everything you need to succeed.

Like many other people, I launched into trading with no plan other than just the idea of wanting to trade shares. After teaching myself the basics I set up an Excel spreadsheet to record my share purchases. Then, armed with a trading plan in my head, I thought I was ready to trade the stock market.

My plan, and probably your plan, was simple — Make A Profit. It sounded like a plan but later I realised it was really a recipe for an emotional roller coaster.

The first stock I bought was a biotechnology stock called Peptech Limited. Within a few days of opening the trade I had a profit and I immediately sold it. Days later, I bought back into the stock for reasons making more sense to me back then than it does now. It was an emotional decision on my part to sell, triggered by the happiness of seeing my first profit and the excitement of making it so quickly. As a beginner trader all I knew was I wanted to make a profit.

Unfortunately, things very rapidly did not go to plan. I needed a more sophisticated plan so I settled on the trading mantras of Profit Good, Loss Bad, and Hold Loss until Profit. What could possibly go wrong?

As it turned out, many things could, and did go wrong. This is the first critical fork in the road for traders. One fork points the way to written trading plans, stop loss, and other apparently non-trading related matters. The other fork, the road most commonly taken, points the way to stock picking. Pick the right stock and you don't need to worry about loss because it's all profit. It's a seductive siren-call leading traders to bankruptcy.

I took the less-travelled fork in the road. The first step was a written trading plan. A written trading plan introduces the essential element of objectivity into our trading for a higher probability of success while removing any emotional reactions from the decision making process. Every trader needs a written plan. It is as essential as a pilot's checklist before takeoff. Every experienced pilot who has flown thousands of times still works with a written checklist for each flight. Everything must be ticked off the list before takeoff.

Successful trading requires the same process and like the checklist for different aircraft, the checklist for every trader is slightly different. However, each checklist has some common similarities. My checklist might not be yours, but it is a starting point for developing your own.

The flight mission checklist for B17 bomber missions used in World War II is equally applicable to trading because the stages of a trade are similar.

(1) Before starting engines      ➔      Before starting TRADE
(2) During warm up               ➔      During LEAD UP TO TRADE
(3) Before takeoff               ➔      Before ENTERING TRADE
(4) During flight                ➔      During TRADE
(5) Before landing               ➔      Before PROFIT/LOSS TARGET
(6) After landing                ➔      After TRADE

A trading plan is a set of rules to guide our trading and behaviour before, during, and after a trade. The summary plan information was mentioned in Chapter 1: Trade Entry Point, Stop Loss Point, and Potential Profit Target. Now we dig deeper.

The plan should also cover the rules on areas such as:

- **Risk management** — This is how much capital we risk and accept losing on each trade. When we are wrong we want to minimise the loss.
- **Money management** — This determines your position size of how many units to buy for a trade and how we manage profits along the way.
- **Stock selection criteria** — Stating the criteria a stock must meet in order to create an objective list of stocks. From this list a final trade is selected.

This is not an exhaustive list of rules but I found it is a good foundation to build on for stock trading or any other instrument you wish to trade. You choose to make your trading plan as simple or as detailed as you want it to be whilst remembering Profit Good, Loss Bad is far too simple.

Pain sears our memory in an area where profits cannot erase. Over the course of this book, I show you how written plans are developed and applied, but first, a little pain is useful to explain why the price of success is eternal written vigilance.

Different methods of trading and different instruments like foreign currencies and derivatives call for a different trading plan. When I first decided to use the ANTSSYS strategy to trade Forex, I wrote in detail the reasons why I would enter a trade and why I would exit a trade. It also included the percentage of my capital I would risk on each trade and how profits would be managed while the trade remained open.

My EURAUD trade illustrates what happened when I didn't have my written trading plan in front of me. I was still functioning in the lazy zone after returning from a holiday break. A few clicks to find and open my trading plan file was just too much trouble after a week of eating good food and where leisurely walks ended in shopping sprees. Having traded this strategy so many times I thought I could manage this trade on autopilot. Instead, I found myself without the discipline of a written plan. I was free to wing it.

The EURAUD short trade is based on the classic ANTSSYS method to capture the maximum number of pips. The ANTSSYS method is covered in Chapter 6.

The ANTSSYS strategy uses an adapted version of the classic GMMA to identify trend and trend changes on a Forex chart. The evolved GMMA has different set values for the moving averages. We see the original long-term GMMA modified to become the Super Guppy and the original short-term GMMA modified to become the Fast Guppy.

Another distinct difference of the ANTSSYS strategy is the use of Range Bar charts. These are charts displaying range bars where the next bar is recorded only when there has been a movement in price. This is different from the traditional price chart where a new bar is printed as each unit of time passes. For this example we don't need the full details but they are discussed in Chapter 25.

We employ a top down analysis where the most suitable highest range bar 7R chart allows us to see a clear picture of the major trend. A medium sized range bar 5R chart helps us confirm the identified trend, and the smallest range bar 3R chart is used to find an entry point to open our trade.

For the EURAUD trade, we used a 7R chart for the long-term time frame, a 5R chart for confirmation of the trend direction on the 7R, and a 3R charts for entry.

The autopilot trading plan I applied was:

Entry 1.4404
Stop 1.4431
Target 1.4365

I quickly scribbled these numbers into a notebook. As far as a written plan was concerned, those were it. The following analysis of my trade describes the trade method used to arrive at these figures.

On the 7R chart, Figure 2.1, the FastGuppy started out on an uptrend before the GMMAs compressed and started projecting a downward direction leading down to the entry point marked by the arrow. The SuperGuppy

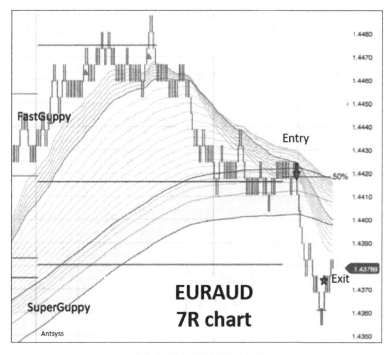

**Figure 2.1.** EURAUD 7R.

had started to turn over to sit above the FastGuppy, a clear reversal of the previous trend and a confirmation of the overall downtrend. The probability of trend continuation is high and further movements of price to the downside are anticipated. We analyse the lower Range Bar charts for a potential short trade.

On the 5R chart, Figure 2.2, the SuperGuppy lines are well separated, showing good support for the emerging downtrend. The FastGuppy shows compression and the start of an expansion of the GMMA lines from the point of the arrow, confirming the general downtrend direction. The 7R and 5R charts are both showing a downtrend. We analyse the lower 3R Range Bar chart for an opportunity to enter a short trade.

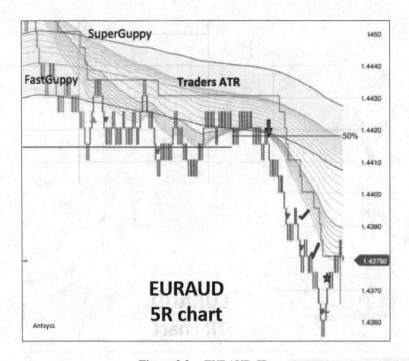

**Figure 2.2.** EURAUD 5R.

On the 3R chart, Figure 2.3, the FastGuppy is compressed at the arrow. We are confident the downtrend has a high probability of continuing based on the confirmation of the 7R and 5R charts. A short trade is opened on the EURAUD at an entry of 1.4404 as marked. Stop Loss is set at 1.4431 as determined by the Traders ATR line above the entry arrow on Figure 2.2, 5R chart. My Take Profit Target is set at 1.4365.

The ticks on the 3R chart show where uneasiness sets in about price reversing. By referring back to the strong supporting evidence of the well-separated GMMA lines on the 5R and 7R charts, we gain some confidence of reaching our profit target.

Now this is where the autopilot gets over-ridden by laziness and greed. A written plan would have quickly exposed the stupidity of this greed reaction.

Moving a target profit level further away as it approaches my set target profit is not part of my autopilot plan but I did it anyway because the trend

**Figure 2.3.** EURAUD 3R.

on the charts looked good. In hindsight my greed and wish for more profit had taken over.

Referring back to the 3R chart, I moved my Take Profit price to 1.4333. Price breaks down through past 1.4389. I thought I was on my way to the new profit target but price retraced back to the top line of the FastGuppy GMMA lines. In order to preserve my open profit, the trade position was closed at 1.4374 at 30 pips.

Had I obeyed the rules of my written trading plan and not allowed my greed to take over, I would have left my original profit target at 1.4365 and a profit would have been achieved at 39 pips. At its lowest price point of 1.4355 on the 3R chart, the maximum potential profit for this trade was for 49 pips. Instead, I traded on autopilot and this failure to properly plan nearly crashed this trade.

As I discovered from painful experience, moving my target profit price during an open trade does not often lead to good results. If I want to chase higher profits then I need to use a trading plan with its own different checklist of rules.

The Bombardier's Information File, issued by the United States Army Air Force in 1945, notes, "It would be more than tragic to subject a bomber and its crew to the hazards of a mission, to consume irreplaceable time reaching the target, and then to discover ... a malfunction prevents the successful accomplishment of ... mission." This is exactly like trading — without checking and adhering to your written trading plan checklist, you might find yourself crashing short of the trading target.

Making a plan and adhering to the rules takes a lot of practice and discipline. B17 flight crews practiced dummy bombing runs for an appallingly low number of hours before putting their lives on the line in missions over Europe. Nowadays flight crews get simulator training and we should too. Many people start with dummy or pretend trading, but I found large and unexpected advantages in taking part in an online game simulating the conditions of buying and selling of shares in a real-time environment.

# Chapter 3

# Not Just a Game

Dummy bombing runs were good enough for B17 pilots, but modern pilots training to fly a giant A380 need sophisticated flight simulators. Likewise, simulated trading is good training for traders even if it's sold as a game. Gaming is not a sideshow. Globally, it's a bigger business than Hollywood. Professional "games" give you confidence in the pilot managing your A380 flight because you know he is well past learning by trial and error.

There are many ways to familiarise ourselves with how the stock market works. Some traders like to choose a trading guru and pay large amounts of money to learn how to trade. Others open a demo account with an online broker or trade in the actual market with small amounts of capital.

Traders who are interested in developing their skills in a more realistic environment may choose to trade against others in the market using a real-time trading simulation. An online stock market trading game is a great starting point. It's easy to set up and a good way to test your trading plans without destroying your hard-earned capital when mistakes are made. Best of all, it's free and it doesn't preclude having some fun.

The Sharemarket Game simulates the Australian stock market environment. It's called a game and it's also a serious training simulation... with a bit of fun on the side. Registered players are given $50,000 in virtual money to create a portfolio of stocks selected from a list of 200 nominated companies. A student pilot is able to make incorrect decisions in simulator flight training without the consequences of a crash and burn. Traders making bad decisions in an online stock simulation also crash but without a real cash burn. Their sense of pride takes a nosedive but not their actual trading capital.

My motivation for entering the Sharemarket Game was to familiarise myself with current trending stocks. This was a test of my ideas about trading and of how I might go about adding trading as an activity to my lifestyle. Finding stock ideas to add to a real-life portfolio whilst having fun doing it also sounded like a good idea.

The Game limits your holding of a stock to 25% of the total portfolio in order to keep the portfolio diversified. The $50,000 did not need to be invested for the entire 15 weeks of the game in order to do well.

Where to start? I chose stocks already in an uptrend on the Weekly chart with well-separated short-term and long-term Guppy Multiple Moving Averages (GMMAs). The selection process involved mainly eye-balling the charts. My eyeballing process involved staring for only a few seconds at individual stocks on a Weekly chart. It's purely a visual process of scanning the GMMAs on the chart. In those few seconds if I saw what I was looking for, the stock would end up on the short list.

Develop your own method of searching for uptrending stocks. Beware of looking too hard and too long because it means your criteria is not there. Move on quickly. The opportunity is either there or it isn't.

Here's one of the lessons learned from this simulation. Success did not depend on jumping in quickly. Time in the market was less important than getting a good entry and good management of the trade. Although the game started in the last week of February, it wasn't until the second week when I bought my first four stocks — BlueScope Steel (BSL), ResMed (RMD), A2 Milk Company (A2M), and Cleanaway Waste (CWY).

A fifth stock, Downer EDI (DOW), was chosen on a random basis, a lazy click based on its early position from the drop-down alphabetical listing. Had I actually bothered to look at the chart I would have seen fantastic looking GMMAs trending up on the Weekly and Daily charts until a recent announce-ment of a capital raising caused the share price to plummet by 20%. The lesson here is to always look at a chart before making your decision to buy.

The simulated trading soon highlighted another lesson. I didn't need to spend much time on a daily basis in monitoring the portfolio. I only checked stock prices and charts every few days or sometimes longer, mak-ing sure the GMMA lines were still in an uptrend and not crashing into one another. This was particularly important on the Weekly charts where the general trend direction of a stock was found. It's only if you use an indicator requiring an exit at an exact stop loss or take profit price would you need to check stock prices more regularly.

Table 3.1 is a summary of my trades during the simulation game.

**Table 3.1.** Simulation game trade summary.

| Code | Date Week No. | Buy Price | Shares | Total | Date Week No. | Sell Price | End of Game Price | Profit/Loss for Shares Sold | Profit/Loss @ Game End 15 Weeks | % Profit |
|------|------|------|------|------|------|------|------|------|------|------|
| BSL | 2 | 12.77 | 974 | 12437.98 | 6 | 11.80 | SOLD | –944.78 | 0 | –7.60% |
| RMD | 2 | 9.49 | 1314 | 12469.86 | 14 | 9.20 | SOLD | –381.06 | 0 | –3.06% |
| A2M | 2 | 2.32 | 5375 | 12470.00 | — | — | 3.25 | 0 | 4998.75 | 40.09% |
| CWY | 2 | 1.25 | 10007 | 12508.75 | — | — | 1.42 | 0 | 1701.19 | 13.60% |
| DOW | 6 | 5.70 | 2024 | 11536.80 | — | — | 6.22 | 0 | 1052.48 | 9.12% |
| ALL | 6 | 20.17 | 496 | 10004.32 | — | — | 22.32 | 0 | 1066.40 | 10.66% |
| | | | | | | | | –1325.84 | 8818.82 | |

Profit/Loss @ Game End **$ 7,492.98**

Cash Reserve 2154.40

**TOTAL PORTFOLIO VALUE** **$ 59,647.38**

* Excluding Dividends

| DIVIDENDS | |
|------|------|
| **CODE** | **AMOUNT** |
| ALL | 69.44 |
| RMD | 40.6 |
| CWY | 100.07 |
| | **210.11** |

These six trades delivered key lessons from this trade training simulation.

## Letting Good Fortune Profits Run — A2M

It's always a great boost for a portfolio to have one of these stocks. A2M, Figure 3.1, was in a strong uptrend on the Weekly and the Daily charts and price rose continuously throughout the game. It was my best performing stock, returning 40% over a 14-week period right up until the end of the game.

Two lessons came from this training exercise. The first was to let profits run. The second was an appreciation of how most trades results are so-so. The bulk of portfolio returns come from just one or two outstanding trades. Learn to recognise them quickly and manage them to maximise profits.

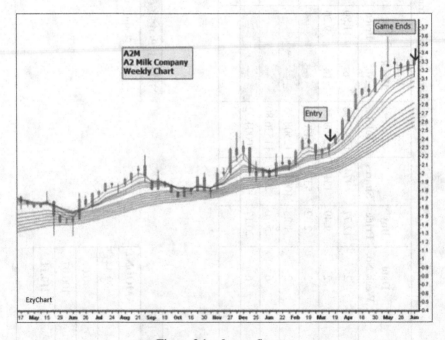

**Figure 3.1.** Let profits run.

## Replacing One Stock for Another — RMD for ALL

I had been checking the Daily chart of RMD, Figure 3.2, regularly and saw the short-term GMMA lines compress and start to turn downwards. Not exactly the price direction I wanted to see in the days following my entry into the stock. Through the twist and turns of the GMMA on the Daily chart I continued to hold my position.

The RMD Weekly chart showed a general uptrend until the short-term GMMA began to also compress and travel sideways, alerting me to the potential of a crash. In order to avoid this, I needed to make a decision to steer clear and change direction. As the trend had turned ugly on the Daily chart of RMD, I sold and replaced this stock with ALL — Aristocrat Leisure.

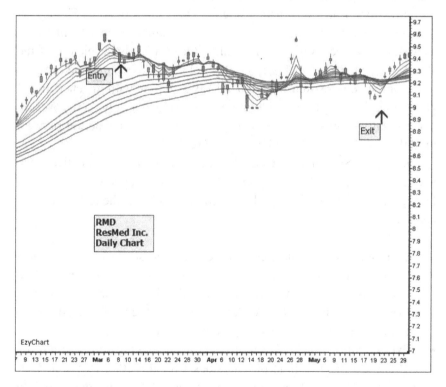

**Figure 3.2.** Sideways trade exit.

Since profit growth in a short period of time was my aim, I sold any underperforming stock and replaced it with another stock exhibiting good profit potential based on the charts. I did this twice in the game without hesitation. It is too easy to delve into a session of self-talk, finding reasons why we should not sell a stock. Hope of the stock turning around and going back in our desired direction is wishful thinking. It prolongs the inevitable and what we know in reality to be true. Make a decision and without another thought, place the order to close your trade. The sooner you do it the smaller your loss. There is nothing more gut-wrenching to a trader than seeing a small loss become an even larger one. Be inspired by the Nike slogan — just do it. Cap your loss and move on. Preserving your capital enables you to continue trading again.

ALL was a much better-looking chart on the Weekly. Both the short-term GMMAs and long-term GMMAs displayed well-separated lines, a sign of a strong well-supported trend by both short-term traders and long-term investors. Entry was made using the Daily chart of ALL, Figure 3.3. The trend was rising and was at a stage of compression. Compression shows an agreement on price and value. Given the bigger picture of the strong uptrend on the Weekly chart, the probability of the uptrend continuing after the compression was high. ALL was in line with my checklist of good trending short-term and long-term GMMAs not only on the Weekly but the Daily chart too. It returned 10.66% over a 16-day period right up until the last day of the simulation exercise.

Playing the Sharemarket Game helped me to experience the live stock market in a non-lethal environment. None of my savings were at risk as I learned how to trade. This simulated trading developed the following concepts and skills.

- **Stock Selection** — The method used to choose stocks to buy. My plan focused on a trend trading strategy where uptrends were identified on a Daily as well as a Weekly chart. The dominant trend direction was always determined by the Weekly chart. Any stocks of interest during the eyeballing process were placed on a shortlist.
- **Diversification** — A 25% rule is enforced making sure you are not risking too much capital on one stock over the other stocks in your portfolio. This is a lesson I carried forward. Although I don't stick to

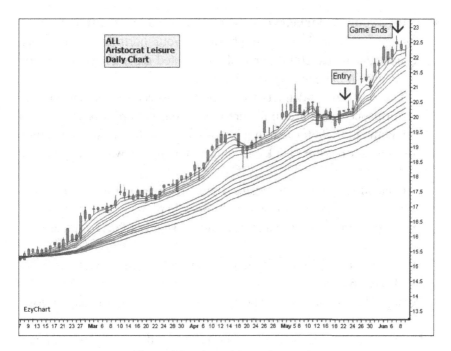

**Figure 3.3.** Assessing trend strength.

a strict 25% rule, I do calculate my risk reward ratio for individual trades ensuring any one loss does not make an impact of more than 2% of my total capital. Generally speaking, I have around 10 stocks at any given time in my portfolio.

- **Real Time Market Experience** — Buy and sell orders are processed in the live market environment during trading hours and include brokerage costs. This is the important difference between a training simulation and a game. The entry or exit price you prefer is not necessarily the price you get.
- **Management of Trades** — When a stock is in profit or loss, decisions need to be made to hold on for longer or to sell. In my regular trading, a sell decision is triggered by a calculated stop loss or when a trade is in profit by a target percentage achieved. In the case of letting profits run past the target profit, a trailing profit stop is employed to preserve as much profit as possible.

- **Gauge your Performance** — Stocks are listed in a portfolio displaying net profit or loss. A graph shows your portfolio performance
  against the Index 200. Your rank is updated daily on your position
  nationally in the game against other players.

  This adds to, or detracts from, the fun aspect, depending on your
  performance. It's a useful feature to see your net profit because when
  you come to trade for real, it's just you against the market so it's only
  the level of your bank account showing how well you are
  performing.

  Comparing yourself to others is great motivation for pushing yourself to achieve more in the game. Those who prefer a consistent benchmark for comparison use a market index. This is a fairer comparison.

Only 46% of players ended the game in profit with an average player
value of $49,964.16.

Perhaps this is the most important lesson of all. Most players lose.
Losing money is easier than making money.

My strategy for the game was fairly straightforward: look for any
stocks trending up using the short-term and long-term GMMAs on the
Daily and Weekly charts. Any stock with a weakness in the trend when the
GMMAs changed direction were sold off and the trade position closed.
This applied to BSL and to RMD during the game. Out of 17, 991 players
nationwide I ended up in the top 1.8%. I was very happy with my end
result as I passed the simulation exam.

The trading game provides a real-time, live environment for players to
test strategies, making it suitable simulation training for both novice and
more experienced traders.

I may never get the opportunity to sit in a flight simulator for an A380,
but using the trading game as a trade training simulator set the foundation
for improving trading performance.

There are thousands of stocks listed on the market. Traders need to cut
this list down to a small pool of trading opportunities. This is often
achieved by defining a set of technical criteria to scan a group of stocks in
order to reduce the list to a manageable number. Luckily, I didn't need to
do this in the sharemarket game because the stock pool was pre-selected
by the organisers.

Simulation is not real life and reducing a list of thousands of stocks to a smaller trade pool takes time, so like everyone else, I am always interested in shortcuts.

I wanted to test a shortcut of using third-party brokerage research for stock ideas. It was also a test of just how accurate or useful these brokerage reports would be in setting up trading strategies. This made the next trading simulation round of the Sharemarket Game an interesting one. Here was an opportunity to test the skills of a co-pilot.

# Chapter 4

# Trading Trading Recommendations

Thousands of stocks are listed on the stock exchange. Assessing each one individually would be a mammoth task for most traders in today's time-poor society. Given that we don't have enough patience or time for sifting through so many stocks, we need to explore other methods to shorten the list.

One common method is for traders to programme their own criteria into a trading platform to perform a data or technical scan. The result is a shorter list of the more interesting stocks. It's like looking for a house. Instead of wasting time trawling through pages of every house on the market, you may only want to see the ones with four bedrooms, two bathrooms, and one garage. A good website enables you to choose your criteria to shorten the list.

These technical scans were very popular when powerful charting programmes first became available. Increasingly, these technical searches have come to rely on higher level mathematical equations more suited to specialists as traders sought even smaller trading advantages in the market. Now stocks pools are created easily by using commonly available search criteria, so the advantages of a technical search are reduced. These pools of technical candidates provide a shortcut for traders looking for trading opportunities.

I'm constantly on high alert for any recommendations of stocks found through finance shows, emails from brokers, or in newspaper and magazine articles. These are great shortcuts to finding stocks doing well in the market. One of my favourite areas for opportunity are stock recommendations where the broker has done all the homework. Like a technical search, which creates a small pool of stocks ready for further analysis.

Combining a broker recommendation with technical analysis increases the probability of choosing a good stock to add to your portfolio. I wanted to explore and see if using this experienced co-pilot was able to guide me to better decisions. For the next round of the Sharemarket Game, I decided to test this method and as a starting point, selected my stocks from a list of broker recommended growth stocks.

## The List

The starting point was a list of growth stocks provided by a financial investment research company. From this list I opened each of the charts and overlaid the short-term GMMA and the long-term GMMA indicators. These formed the foundation of my own criteria in determining the trending stocks most likely to rise further in price. I searched for stocks using Daily charts where the short-term GMMA lines were trending up and sitting above the long-term GMMA lines, moving in the same upward direction. The second requirement was for these GMMA lines to be found in the same order for an uptrend on the Weekly chart too. Whenever I found stocks where both the Weekly chart and the Daily chart met my criteria, I would see these GMMA lines as high probability rainbows leading to a possible pot of trading gold.

I brought up each chart from the broker's growth stocks list and went through the process of eyeballing one chart after another until the group was reduced to a handful of the most promising stocks. The final stocks chosen were Fisher and Paykel Healthcare Corp (FPH), Integrated Research Limited (IRI), Regis Resources (RRL), and Sandfire Resources (SFR).

## The Strategy

I applied a buy and hold strategy throughout the game. It was tempting to cull any losers and replace them. Instead I decided to wait and see if these broker-recommended growth stocks could return any profits over the 15 weeks of the Sharemarket Game. Seedlings don't grow into trees overnight so why do we expect to see stocks grow mega profits in just one day? Don't get me wrong I would love to see a stock double its share price over a week. I am a realist to my core so I don't look for the "Get Rich Quick" strategies. The stocks in the portfolio needed some time to develop. All stocks were checked a few times during the game at random intervals so the time spent monitoring the portfolio were minimal.

Given the shorter time frame for the game, the measure of success was the performance of the stock rather than the time in the market. The results in this selection are consistent with the results achieved when this strategy has been applied subsequently.

## The Best Performer

Out of all the stocks, the best performer was SFR. This stock returned a profit of 17.68% over 15 weeks to the last day of the game.

On the Weekly chart, Figure 4.1, both the short-term group and the long-term group of moving averages show good separation and are

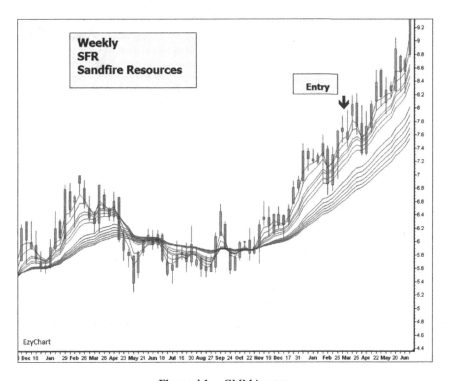

**Figure 4.1.** GMMA entry.

travelling in the same upwards direction. The degree of separation in the long-term GMMA shows strong support by investors for the uptrend in place. This relationship is an essential precondition for inclusion in my stock pool.

On the Daily chart, Figure 4.2, the lines of the short-term GMMA have recently compressed and expanded. Compression signalled an agreement on price and value by traders before the expansion showed price starting to rise. The future is one of potential, for further price rises and is a good signal against the background of the stable uptrend seen on the Weekly chart. The Weekly chart provides us with a bigger picture of the primary trend in place. Trading with the trend keeps us in a trade for longer.

Based on the uptrend of the Weekly chart, a decision was made to open a trade using the Daily chart. An entry was made at $7.58 as marked.

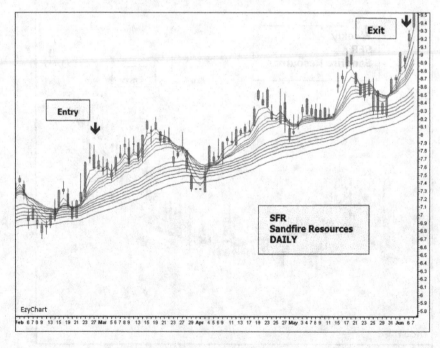

**Figure 4.2.** Best trade outcome.

## The Worst Performer

Out of all the stocks, the worst performer was IRI. This stock returned a loss of 10.10% over 15 weeks to the last day of the game.

On the Weekly chart of IRI, Figure 4.3, the well-separated lines of the long-term GMMA showed support for the underlying uptrend up to the point of entry as marked by the arrow. Compression of the short-term moving averages shows an agreement on price by buyers and sellers. The general trend was up and I saw this compression area as a point of price weakness, a mid-trend entry. It was an opportunity to join an existing uptrend.

I wasn't too concerned about the compression of the short-term GMMA or the sideways price movement as this was after all a growth stock for growth over the long-term. However, we need to be careful not to use this as an excuse for staying with a poorly performing stock.

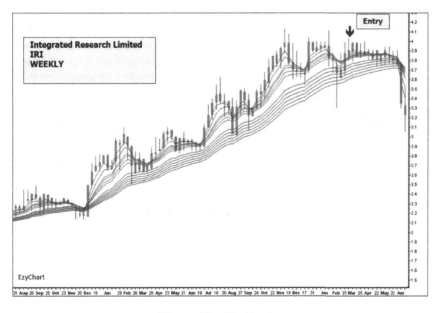

**Figure 4.3.**   Rapid exit.

On the Daily chart, Figure 4.4, leading up to the point of entry as marked by the arrow, the lines of the short-term GMMA had recently compressed and expanded moving up through the long-term GMMA. The lines of the long-term GMMA were not impressive as the long-term investors were not showing much interest in this stock for the long term.

As this was a Daily chart, I was willing to overlook this because my decision was based on the uptrend of the Weekly chart. An entry was made at $3.86 as marked. My exit at $3.47 on the last day of the game is also marked on the chart. Admittedly, the lines of the GMMAs on the daily were not picture perfect. A wider separation of the long-term GMMA lines showing stronger investor support would have been preferred. I chose to accept the rising expansion of trader activity represented by the short-term GMMA as sufficient evidence of future upwards price movements. After opening, the trade price chose to travel mostly sideways. The short-term GMMA eventually emerged from the sideways tangle to slide into position under the long-term GMMA lines. It was the start of a

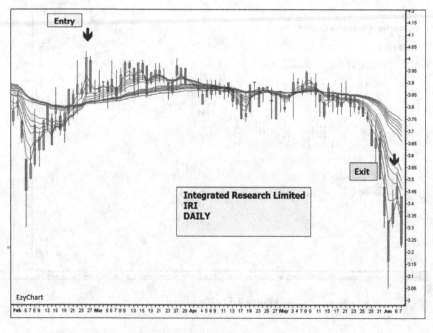

**Figure 4.4.** Delayed exit decision.

definite downtrend. A ray of hope appeared in the last few days when price finished up 9.7% in two days yet price was still technically in a downtrend. This trade in IRI demonstrates how deviating from ideal conditions may reduce your probability of success in the right direction.

## Final Outcome

On the last day of the game, 57% of players were in profit. My final overall ranking was 1,432 out of 16,830 players nationally, placing me in the top 8%. My portfolio low of the game was $49,903.33 and my portfolio high during the game was $54,256.12.

Table 4.1 summarises the profits and losses of the game.

Three out of the four stocks chosen showed some growth over the course of the game. Two returned double-digit figures. The worst performer has only a single digit lower return but was more profitable than cash sitting in the bank. IRI didn't deliver as a growth stock and its chart was looking more like a downtrend.

Of course, the brokers' response to a collapsing price is often "hold on", this is an investment, not a trade. Twelve months later, the IRI price bottomed around $1.57 and after a slow rebound, clambered painfully back to $2.70, some 30% below the trading game entry price of $3.86. Investor or trader, you cannot afford to wait 12 months or more for your position to become profitable. It is a poor use of your capital.

Brokers are often seen as the ones with the crystal ball but they are not any wiser than you or me in predicting what the price of a share could possibly be in the future. Armed with skills in technical analysis, we make our own decisions and are steps ahead of the average broker-based investor if we are able to read the charts to know what the stock is doing and to trade with the overall trend.

It's not all bad news when it comes to brokers. There is some value in using a third-party broker selected stock pool. Good fundamentals ensure high quality candidates for us to choose from. Link this with good technicals and we have a standout stock worth having a closer look at. Be wary though of relying too heavily on fundamentals for decision-making. The price decline in IRI and the double-digit growth for RRL and SFR were not forecast by brokerage fundamentals. Technical analysis triumphs over

Table 4.1. Game profit and loss report.

| Code | Date Week No. | Buy Price | Shares | Total | End of Game Price | Profit/Loss @ Game End 15 Weeks | % Profit |
|---|---|---|---|---|---|---|---|
| FPH | 2 | 12.49 | 1000 | 12490.00 | 13.26 | 770.00 | 6.16% |
| IRI | 2 | 3.86 | 3223 | 12440.78 | 3.47 | -1256.97 | -10.10% |
| RRL | 2 | 4.29 | 2901 | 12445.29 | 4.88 | 1711.59 | 13.75% |
| SFR | 2 | 7.58 | 1645 | 12469.10 | 8.92 | 2204.30 | 17.68% |
| | | | | 49845.17 | | 3428.92 | |

| | |
|---|---|
| Profit/Loss @ Game End | $ 3,428.92 |
| Cash Reserve | 422.73 |
| **TOTAL PORTFOLIO VALUE** | **$ 53,851.65** |
| Including Dividends | $ 54,215.33 |

| DIVIDENDS | |
|---|---|
| CODE | AMOUNT |
| RRL | 232.08 |
| SFR | 131.60 |
| | **363.68** |

fundamentals as it enables us to make our own informed decisions without needing constant advice from a broker.

Having an experienced co-pilot didn't provide the performance boost I expected. It was a good way of quickly creating a smaller pool of trading opportunities, but it didn't bring a clear advantage. This strategy provided one important lesson. It was clear even to a child that the IRI chart was not showing strong trend behaviour and should have been avoided. If the chart analysis does not support the broker analysis, then you had better believe the chart.

Perhaps it's time to ditch the experienced co-pilot in favour of a simpler view? In the next chapter, we test one final strategy using the Sharemarket Game. We literally pass the trade plan to a child to determine if a younger, less experienced co-pilot could succeed by using a very simple trading plan.

# Chapter 5

# Child's Play

In 2009, Northwest Airlines Flight 188 overshot their destination by more than 240 km due to pilot distraction. Both pilot and co-pilot were busy on their laptops. Distractions keep us from focusing on the task in front of us, whether we are flying or trading. I also plead guilty to this. Hunting for food in the cupboard or opening an extra browser tab for yet another interesting website is a distracting displacement activity distracting us from real work. It won't lead to a potential airline disaster, but it certainly won't help us find the next trade.

Traders are subject to many distractions both externally and within the charts. We might be influenced in our decision-making and trade management by the latest news report on a company or by every bump and dip in the share price during the day.

Distractions eat away at trade discipline. Distractions make a simple trade plan more complex than necessary. Distractions sabotage our ability and they often come from our deep subconscious — but no need to examine or resolve them here. Better to develop harm minimisation strategies. We often think we could trade better without these distractions so I tested this approach in the next round of the Sharemarket Game by engaging a truly disinterested third party.

I enlisted Justin, the 14-year-old son of a neighbourhood friend, to play the game using one simple strategy. I gave him the freedom to make decisions on the stocks to buy and sell. Without any fundamental knowledge and minimal technical analysis skills, the only rule he followed was to choose stocks trending up on the Weekly chart using the short-term and long-term GMMAs. This is a very simple trading plan, so he did not suffer from the distractions that come from the news, from multiple chart analysis methods, and from the fear of making or losing money.

## The List

Justin started with a list of 200 stocks predetermined by the game organisers. He used the eyeball method to determine the stocks he saw as trending up on the Weekly chart with the potential for further upward price movements. The stocks chosen were A2 Milk (A2M), Qantas (QAN), Mineral Resources (MIN), Costa Group Holdings (CGC), and Treasury Wine Estates (TWE). An exception to the rule was Sydney Airport (SYD) chosen simply because he liked it. This one departure from the trade strategy delivered the lowest profit.

## The Strategy

Justin used a buy and hold strategy throughout the game. The only exceptions were the two stocks QAN and SYD because they did not meet his price momentum expectations. Compared to the other stocks he had chosen, these two stocks appeared to be travelling nowhere. He gave up on them and they were sold during the game. All stocks were checked a few times a week after the close of trade, so the time spent monitoring the portfolio was minimal.

## The Best Performer

We look at just one example taken from this undistracted approach. It may be the best of the bunch, but as the summary results show, this profitable trade was by no means an unusual result for this approach. It took a while to recruit Justin, so he placed his first order 48 days after the start of the game. Out of all the stocks, the best performer was Costa Group Holdings — CGC. This stock returned 29% over 54 days to the last day of the game.

CGC was identified by Justin as an uptrending stock on the Weekly chart and an entry was made as marked by the up arrow.

On the CGC Weekly chart, Figure 5.1, both the short-term group and the long-term group of moving averages showed good separation and were travelling in the same upwards direction. Both the long-term investors and the short-term traders were supporting this trend. The lines of the short-term GMMA were sitting above the lines of the long-term GMMA in an order confirming the uptrend in place. This chart exhibits the criteria Justin required for determining whether a stock was trending and likely to continue to do so in the future.

At the time of entry, the Daily chart of CGC, Figure 5.2, was showing sideways price movement in the short-term GMMA. Not long afterwards, price broke out of this range and began to move upwards. The short-term

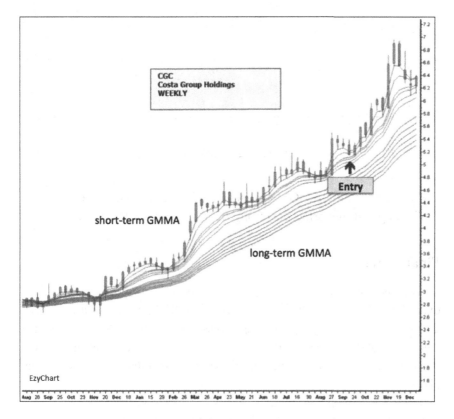

**Figure 5.1.** GMMA entry.

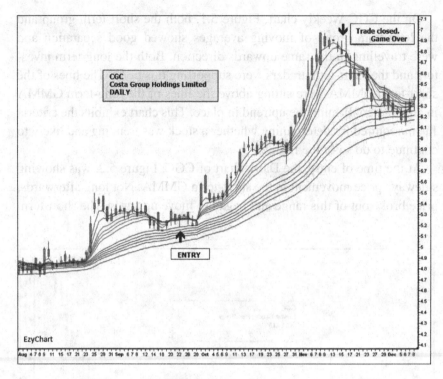

**Figure 5.2.**    Trade exit.

GMMA and long-term GMMA began to separate and slope upwards, confirming and mirroring the strong trend lines of the Weekly chart.

## Final Outcome

On the last day of the game, 84% of players were in profit. Justin's final overall ranking was in the top 7% out of 16,830 players nationally. His portfolio low of the game was $50,008 and portfolio high during the game was $60,459. But remember, this result is achieved after entering just only halfway through the game! Avoiding distractions pays excellent dividends.

Table 5.1 summarises Justin's profits and losses in the game.

Success in the Sharemarket Game in this case study was a result of identifying good trending stocks and avoiding the distractions of news and

**Table 5.1.** Trading game results.

| Code | Date Week No. | Buy Price | Shares | Total | Date Week No. | Sell Price | End of Game Price | Profit/Loss for Shares Sold | Profit/Loss @ Game End 15 Weeks | % Profit |
|---|---|---|---|---|---|---|---|---|---|---|
| A2M | 7 | 5.40 | 2327.00 | 12565.80 | — | — | 6.84 | 0 | 3350.88 | 26.67% |
| QAN | 7 | 5.88 | 2124.00 | 12489.12 | 8 | 5.76 | SOLD | −254.88 | 0 | −2.04% |
| MIN | 7 | 15.51 | 798.00 | 12376.98 | — | — | 18.02 | 0 | 2002.98 | 16.18% |
| CGC | 7 | 5.25 | 2376.00 | 12474.00 | — | — | 6.78 | | 3635.28 | 29.14% |
| SYD | 10 | 7.12 | 1713.00 | 12196.56 | 10 | 7.24 | SOLD | 205.56 | 0 | 1.69% |
| TWE | 12 | 14.93 | 827.00 | 12347.11 | — | — | 15.6 | 0 | 554.09 | 4.49% |
| | | | | | | | | −49.32 | 9543.23 | |

Profit/Loss
@ Game End $ 9,493.91

Cash Reserve 5.88

**TOTAL PORTFOLIO VALUE** $ 59,499.79

over-analysis. For Justin, a simple strategy based on finding uptrends on the Weekly chart with good short-term and long-term GMMAs produced a profitable and high yielding portfolio. All the information required to see and assess the uptrend was on the chart.

Using only the GMMA indicator was enough and proved to be a quick way of identifying the overall trend. If a child could see it then it was obvious. As traders, we sometimes look too hard and for too long at a chart — an overanalysis distraction. If the trend is not immediately obvious then it means the trend is not there. We should move onto more probable and profitable opportunities.

Buried in these results is a nugget turning out to be more important than almost everything else I learned from these three simulations. This nugget is hidden in plain sight and we intend to polish it in later chapters. For now, just note for future reference the size of the very small loss on the QAN trade.

This is an extreme approach, tested in real-time conditions against other traders using more complex trading strategies. The results show how distractions are a hindrance in more ways than one. In the last three chapters, we looked at a variety of trading strategies, all applied in a simulated trading game environment competing against skilled traders and using real-time market data.

The results told me simplicity is important, but it is not the complete answer. The results told me I could transfer the task of selecting a stock pool to a third party but the responsibility for the trade success or failure remained with me. These three game simulations gave me confidence in the foundations of my trading approach and opened the way to investigating how other strategies may be applied.

In the next chapter, we explore a strategy incorporating a few more indicators evolved from these game studies. Trading this method requires some new skills and an alternative way of managing profits along the way.

# Chapter 6

# Trading Between the Lines

A starting point on the road to successful trading is looking for an indicator or combination of indicators to produce lots of winning trades. Some traders look for complex strategies but I prefer to keep the strategy simple.

So far in this book, the main strategy has involved only one indicator, the GMMA, and one equity market. In putting together a more complete trading plan, we now combine the GMMA with one other feature. These are Support and Resistance lines. We call this strategy ANTSSYS 321. We set a profit target and set a Stop Loss price too as these are useful bits of information for setting boundaries around the trade. They tell us where we Take Profits and where to get out if we are wrong.

Support and resistance levels are one of the basic principles of technical analysis often used successfully by many traders. These levels give additional information for analysing price and work well when combined with any given strategy.

Support and Resistance lines drawn on a chart are levels where price often pauses and reacts. When price does breakthrough the level, it sets the scenario for further measured price movement and a price target.

The chart in Figure 6.1 shows three lines drawn at 76.00, 75.90, and 75.70. Marking these lines on your chart make it more obvious as to where price has paused and reacted in the past. The story of price on this chart extract unfolds by following price movements from A to C. Around area A, sellers came into the market to drive the price of the stock down to the 75.70 price level three times. Sellers were overcome by the buyers with each attempt. When the 75.70 price level was reached, more buyers came into the market pushing the stock price back up as the demand for

**Figure 6.1.** Support and Resistance lines.

the stock rose while the sellers were unable to keep up with the supply of stock. The overwhelming response of buyers resulted in price being unable to break down through the support level at 75.70. A support level forms when buyers frequently enter into the market at a particular price level to push the price of a stock upwards.

On the fourth attempt to break the support around area A, buyers came into the market again and helped push the price up to the next level at 75.90. At the 75.90 level, the sellers pushed price back down and buyers continued to push price up to 75.90 many times. A resistance line is drawn across the chart showing price reaching this level and then being rejected. A rejection is where price moves higher but then falls back to close lower. The attempt to push price higher is "rejected".

Notice the spikes of rejection above this line just before area B. Each rejection spike is where sellers entered into the market pushing price back down to close under 75.90. Buyers were unable to push price higher beyond the upper limit. A few more attempts and price eventually breaks up past 75.90 and hits the next resistance level at 76.00 as marked by area B. From this level, price bounces off the 76.00 level, turning down and passing through the next support/resistance level at 75.90. Price continues its downwards trajectory then bounces up off the next support/resistance level at 75.70, area C. Support and Resistance levels on a chart are useful for making decisions on entry, exit, and Target Profit prices.

Support and Resistance are a critical part of the ANTSSYS 321 strategy. This is a short-term strategy designed for trading specifically in the Forex market. There are many traders in Forex who like to make a profit in a big way for every trade. Aiming for a large profit on each trade also equates to a large loss if price fails to go in the desired direction. It's the fastest way to zero, or worse, in your trading account if you don't really know what you're doing. My main goal for each ANTSSYS 321 trade is to take a profit of 30 pips. It is based on the idea of building wealth by adding to your trading capital regularly through many small trades.

You may scoff at the thought of smaller profits but the reality is it really does add up. Think of the suggestions often made by financial money experts when it comes to saving money. They tell us cutting down on a $20 per week coffee habit at Starbucks on the way to work equates to a saving of approximately $20 × 48 weeks, $1,000 per year. Translating this concept to Forex profits, if we managed 30 pips × $5 per pip successful trades three times a week for 50 weeks then by the end of one year we would end up with a total profit of $22,500. Not bad for a supplementary income.

Support and Resistance levels observed on a price chart provide good reference points when used in combination with the ANTSSYS 321 strategy. These levels provide additional evidence for a number of scenarios where uncertainty exists. We cannot predict with certainty where price goes to or where price might pause or bounce. Drawing Support and Resistance levels gives us high probability areas where price might pause. This information is especially useful in calculating Target Profits or profit taking exit points when in profit. It is also a method for assessing how many resistance barriers stand in the way of achieving our Target Profit.

I use support and resistance price levels to help determine whether my Target Profit is likely to be achieved as well as for entry and exit points in a trade.

Once we identify good trending GMMA lines we are sitting on a rainbow, hopeful of a correct analysis and finding the pot of gold sooner than later. Price doesn't move smoothly in one direction until it gets to the pot of gold at the end. Without notice, a complete change in trend direction is possible before reaching our Target Profit. Less adventurous traders may wish to lock in some profits from an open trade as part of their strategy.

Support and Resistance levels on a chart provide useful price levels to mine some of the gold nuggets scattered along the way.

When trading stocks I normally use the more common form of chart based on time. If for example I am looking at a 4-hour chart, a price bar is plotted for each passing 4-hour time period. For the ANTSSYS 321 strategy, another form of chart known as range bar charts are used. Details of the range bar charts are discussed in Chapter 25, but for this example, we just need to focus on the Support and Resistance levels which are the same on any type of chart display.

When trading FX using the ANTSSYS 321 strategy I often use a 7-pip range bar chart (7R), a 5-pip range bar chart (5R), and a 3-pip range bar chart (3R) to analyse a potential trade. For the 7R chart, a price bar is plotted for every 7-pip movement in price. If price moves less than 7 pips, no bar is plotted on the chart. A 5R chart requires price to move 5 pips before a bar is plotted and a 3R chart requires price to move 3 pips before a bar is plotted.

For this trade, I used three range bar charts: 7R for the general trend direction, 5R for the confirmation of trend, and 3R for the entry chart. In assessing a potential trade opportunity for a short-term price movement, these three different range bar charts should preferably be trending in the same direction. This similar to Elder Triple Screen trading method.

The Elder Triple Screen trading method uses three timeframes for trading. When all three timeframes are in agreement of the trend direction, the probability of a successful trade is increased. We analyse three time frames charts to determine and confirm the trend direction.

(1) **Long-term trend** — It is the main chart in determining the overall trend direction. For example, a Weekly chart where each candle represents one week. This is the 7R chart.
(2) **Intermediate trend** — It is a shorter timeframe chart from the long-term trend chart. It is the chart we are trading from. For example, a Daily chart where each candle represents one day. This is the 5R chart.
(3) **Short-term trend** — It is a shorter timeframe chart from the intermediate trend chart used to determine our entry into a trade. For example, a 1-hour chart where each candle represents one hour. This is the 3R chart.

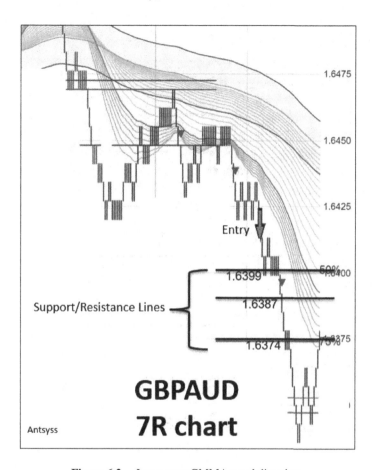

**Figure 6.2.** Long-term GMMA trend direction.

On the 7R chart, Figure 6.2, the lines of the short-term GMMA are projecting in a downwards direction leading up to the entry point, as marked by the arrow. Further downside movement is anticipated. The lines of the long-term GMMA are sitting above the short-term GMMA. This indicates a change in the general trend direction from up to down, adding further probability of price continuation downwards.

On the 5R chart, Figure 6.3, the long-term GMMA lines are well separated, showing good support for the emerging downtrend. The short-term GMMA sitting below the long-term GMMA showed some compression

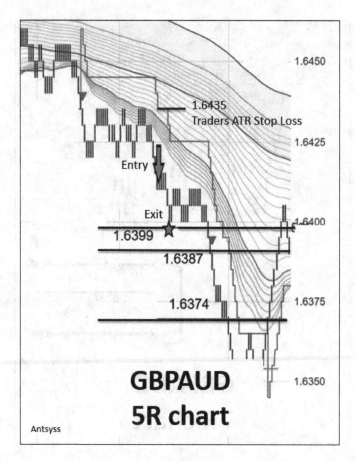

**Figure 6.3.** Confirmation of long-term chart.

and sideways movement then began a downward expansion. As the lines of the short-term GMMA begin to separate and slope down, it confirms the general downtrend direction of this range bar chart. The downtrend is in line with the 7R chart.

On the left side of the 3R chart, Figure 6.4, my entry chart, the short-term GMMA has compressed and the long-term GMMA lines sitting above have separated. This chart is in the early stage of a downtrend and is in line with the trend of the 7R and 5R charts.

The GMMA analysis tells us about the trend. The next step in this trade method is to identify the Support and Resistance levels.

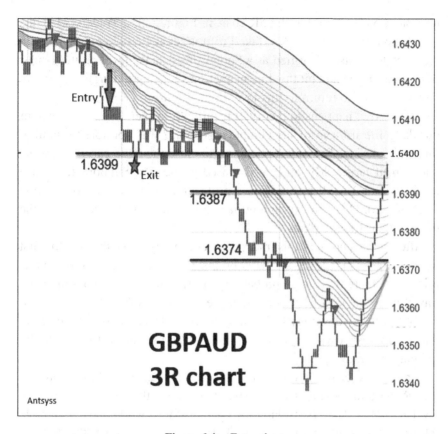

**Figure 6.4.**   Entry chart.

The major Support/Resistance lines are identified by analysing a
1-hour candlestick chart based on price. Using a chart based on price
shows the full range of price action in detail. Bars are plotted more frequently than shown on the range bar chart, and this enables easier identification of obvious Support and Resistance lines. In comparison, the
simpler range bar chart reduces the noise of price activity and is not as
ideal. The 1-hour price chart I analysed for this is not shown but the three
relevant Support/Resistance levels are plotted at 1.6399, 1.6387, and
1.6374. These are marked on the 3R chart as well as the earlier 5R and 7R
charts.

I opened a short trade on the GBPAUD at 1.6413 as marked by the
arrow on the 3R chart. The Traders ATR is used to set a Stop Loss in order

to protect our capital. On the 5R chart in Figure 6.3, a Traders ATR line set a Stop Loss at 1.6435. My Take Profit is set at 1.6387 coinciding with the price level also identified as a Support/Resistance level on the 1-hour price chart. Price had hit this line many times making it a high probability target for price to return to this level in the future.

Life is what happens to theory. It is difficult to spend every moment of our daily life in front of the computer screen. I was not able to monitor this trade closely. The only option was to close the trade early before the Take Profit target. My trade was closed at the first Support/Resistance level price of 1.6399 resulting in a profit of 14 pips and personal stress level of zero. Other traders might have let the trade run according to the rules of their trading plans.

After the exit point of this trade, price eventually broke through the first Support/Resistance level at 1.6399 on the 3R chart, Figure 6.4. From this price point there was a high probability of price movement continuing and travelling to the next Support/Resistance level of 1.6387. Price continued to move further downwards to this next price level easily. The original Take Profit target was achieved. A result of 26 pips of profit for a trader holding this trade open.

When price broke through the Support/Resistance level at 1.6387 on the 3R chart, the next logical price point target was the Support/Resistance level at 1.6374. Traders still holding open positions would have seen price fall further to reach this level of 1.6374. Closing the trade at this point is a result of 36 pips in profit.

Support and Resistance levels show how many price levels must be overcome before reaching a Target Profit. If there are too many then maybe the Target Profit is very difficult to attain. Combined with the ANTSSYS 321 strategy, the additional confirmation provided by these levels was an essential element in assessing further price movements and determining the probability of success.

Planning accommodation and airfares for a holiday without a destination is futile. When we plan a trade we need a Target Profit in order to determine the steps in our trading plan. The next chapter explores the Support and Resistance concept further and discusses how these play a role in planning profit targets.

Many traders focus on the entry price of their trade. Important as it is for achieving the best price, paying attention to the other end of the trade and knowing your Target Profit also contributes to the planning of a successful trade because it puts numbers on the risk/reward calculation. Knowing what you're aiming for helps develop a trading plan to achieve the end goal.

Every runner trains according to an end goal. Training schedules vary according to whether the goal is a 5 kilometre, 10 kilometre, half marathon, or full marathon run. A training plan for a 5-kilometre run may not enable you to run the 21-kilometre half marathon easily. A trading plan to capture 50 pips may not enable you to capture 100 pips easily. Before opening a trade it's good to know what your end goal is. The trading plan for a 50-pip trade is not going to be the same as the trading plan for a 100-pip one. Once you predetermine what your goal is then plan your trade strategy accordingly.

There is the potential to take a smaller profit when price reaches the target price in a 50-pip trade. Sometimes an exit delay would mean taking a larger profit as price continues on or a larger loss for a trade triggering a Stop Loss. Dealing with this variation of greed is discussed in Chapters 13 and 29.

We do not achieve success by chance or by simply clicking a button to open the trade hoping for the best. By working within the ANTSSYS 321 framework, we know 30-pip trades are achievable.

Capping a loss or holding for more profit is a decision up to the individual trader. For a longer-term trader with a target of 100 pips, the rise and fall of price by 20 pips is easily accommodated in a long-term trade plan but for the shorter-term trader time is shorter. The short-term trader aiming for 30 pips cannot afford to play the waiting game for too long. In the case of those trading in the Australian time zone, it means delaying bedtime and getting less sleep.

Once the short- or long-term nature of a trade is known, decide on the charts appropriate for analysis. Using the relevant charts also helps in setting a realistic Take Profit and Stop Loss. Together with the entry price these are the main elements required for assembling a plan to reach the end goal. In the ANTSSYS 321 case, the goal of 30 pips.

Just as a race distance demands an appropriate training plan, an end goal of 100 pips requires a different trading plan than the 30-pip plan discussed above. It needs a longer timeframe and a wider Stop Loss.

On my computer monitor, the sight of pips ticking further into my favour have often tempted me to move the Target Profit to accommodate my mirage of more profit ahead. This is not always a good idea. Discipline in following the original trading plan is the better strategy for continued success. Changing the goal to 100 pips whilst in a 24-pip trading plan is just wishful thinking.

As demonstrated, Support and Resistance levels identified on a chart are useful in our trading for assessing the probability of achieving a Target Profit. In turn it helps us decide on the better option of closing or holding on longer to our open positions. In the next chapter, we look at the easily identifiable round number Support and Resistance levels.

# Chapter 7

# Big, Round, and Probable

Going once, going twice ... SOLD at $1,450,000! During a live house auction, a leading bidder was reluctant to increase his bid by $1,000 to make it $1,451,000, resulting in the sold price of $1,450,000 to the nearest competitor. We just love round numbers; 50, 100, 120. Auction results of properties sold are more often than not the prices ending with nice round numbers. These are levels where buyers, sellers, and price seem to naturally agree and intersect. Much the same is seen in trading as it is similar to the continuous bidding at an auction. The big figure numbers and the round numbers can provide high probability areas to enter or exit a trade.

In practical terms, it means a Support or Resistance level is more likely to be at $10.00 than at $10.14.

Support and Resistance levels are often incorporated into the trading plans. Price tends to either stop and bounce off these levels or pass through these areas to reach new targets as buyers and sellers place orders around these psychological areas. Finding Support and Resistance levels at round numbers provides added probability of price reacting once this figure is reached.

In the following GBPUSD trade, a round figure of 1.3000 is identified as a Support/Resistance level found on the Daily chart. The trade plan is built around this round number.

We introduce a different trade method in this chapter, a Price Action strategy often used in FX as well as in stock trading. A Price Action strategy uses chart patterns and movements in price to identify high probability trade opportunities. No other technical indicators are used. Our entry decision, management of the trade, and exit decision are based purely on price. The starting method of our analysis uses the Elder Triple Screen trading method.

Using a top down multiple time frame analysis, the starting point for this trade is the Daily chart, looking for anything of interest suggesting the future direction of the trend. The Daily chart of GBPUSD, Figure 7.1, shows price moving in a downwards direction. A horizontal line of Support/Resistance is drawn across the chart at the 1.3000 price level. At the right side of the chart, we see price tried to push up through the resistance line at 1.3000 unsuccessfully. A bounce off the 1.3000 line sees price move down again. Turning our attention to a lower timeframe enables us to further investigate the details of Price Action, in this case specifically the retreat 1.3000.

On the GBPUSD 1-hour chart, the focus is on the far right side of what was seen on the previous Daily chart (see Figure 7.1). The bounce away from the resistance line at 1.3000 is seen in more detail as a double top on the 1-hour chart as marked by the two down arrows. This confirms price wants to move down. A trendline is drawn. We look for price to break the trendline before we consider it as a trade opportunity. In order to get even closer to what price is doing, we look to a lower timeframe down for a possible entry.

**Figure 7.1.** GBPUSD Daily chart.

**Figure 7.2.**   GBPUSD 1-hour chart.

The 5-minute chart, Figure 7.3, is our Entry chart. At the right side of this chart is a large down arrow pointing over the right side area of the double top seen on the 1-hour chart in Figure 7.2. Price has broken through the trendline with a back end retest of the line, signalling an entry. At the point where price retests the trendline, we immediately open a short trade on GBPUSD at the entry price of 1.2857. A Stop Loss is set at 1.2880 and a Take Profit price set at 1.2831.

A backend retest is where price retraces back to a level, in this case a trendline, to retest the line. If it is a successful backend retest, price touches the trendline, turns around, and moves away from the line towards our Target Profit. If the backend retest fails, price approaches the line to test it and instead of stopping to turn, continues to move through the trendline in the direction away from our Take Profit target.

On the 5-minute chart, Figure 7.4, immediately after opening the trade we see price moves down then back up again through the diagonal trendline. A micro double top forms, as marked by the two smaller down arrows. The formation of this bearish pattern signals a high probability of price resuming its movement down in the direction of our trade. Price moves down and reaches the Take Profit price of 1.2831. A profit of 26 pips.

**Figure 7.3.**    GBPUSD 5-minute entry chart.

**Figure 7.4.**    GBPUSD 5-minute chart.

Support and Resistance levels are good areas to identify on a chart as a starting point for a trading plan. They become more interesting and meaningful when they also correlate to a round figure number. This tends to make the probability of price movement and possible profits even greater.

Round figures help define the parameters of the trade. They help you decide on the more probable exit targets levels and they often confirm the correct placement of Support and Resistance levels.

Closing a short-term trade doesn't necessarily mean the end of trading. The same chart has the potential to give traders another opportunity to enter into a new trade in the same stock or currency pair with the possibility of another profitable trade. This double dipping often uses a new set of figures and we look at this strategy in the next chapter.

# Chapter 8

# Double Dipping

In Western society, "double dipping" is seen as a social faux pax. Dipping a chip into a food dip after having already taken a bite is generally frowned upon. Not necessarily so when it comes to trading. It is possible, and often profitable, to return for a second dip even after you have already taken a bite out of the trade.

The following GBDCAD trade is used to demonstrate the "double dipping" concept. Building upon the concept of ANTSSYS 321 first described in Chapter 6, we modify the strategy in order to pick up more pips during broader market moves. Changing the long-term range bar chart to a higher range enables us to do this.

For this trade, I used a 10R chart for the long-term time frame to determine the general trend direction, the 5R chart for medium-term confirmation of the direction on the 10R, and a 3R chart for my entry.

On the 10R chart, Figure 8.1, the short-term GMMA has compressed in the area marked by the first down arrow on the left, Trade 1. The long-term GMMA is well separated, showing good long-term investor support for the downtrend to continue. Further downside movement is anticipated.

We look for an entry point on the 3R chart, Figure 8.2. The earlier compression of the short-term GMMA before the area at Trade 1 showed traders were at a point of agreement on price. Price broke out in a downward direction while the lines of the short-term GMMA expanded, crossing down through the long-term GMMA. With the short-term GMMA lines sitting beneath the long-term GMMA lines, they are in the correct order of a downtrend. The 3R chart is in line with the downtrend of the 10R charts.

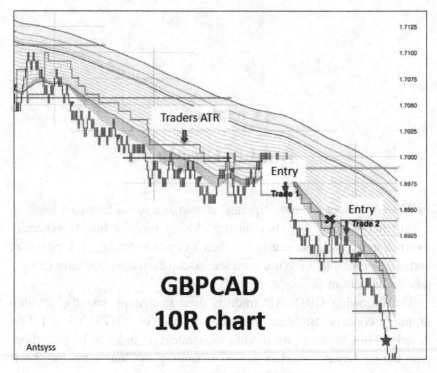

**Figure 8.1.** GBPCAD 10R chart.

Based on the high probability of trend continuation, an entry for Trade 1 is made as marked by the down arrow on the 3R chart. A short position was opened at 1.6960 and a Profit Target of 1.6821 was set based on Support and Resistance lines identified on a 1-hour price chart.

When aiming for more pips and trading broader market moves, a Traders ATR on the longer-term chart is preferred for managing the trade. A Stop Loss of 1.7012 was calculated by referencing the Traders ATR line on the 10R chart, Figure 8.1. The Traders ATR is discussed in more detail in Chapter 24. In this example, we just need to know that the line acts as a Stop Loss trigger. As Trade 1 moved into profit, the Traders ATR was used as a trailing Stop Loss to manage the trade in order to protect profit. My rules for trading FX prevent me from trading during news announcements. By referencing a Forex calendar, I was aware of the upcoming

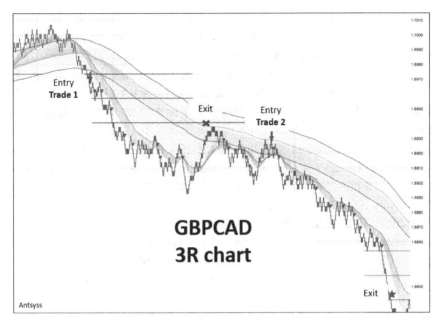

**Figure 8.2.** GBPCAD 3R chart.

news announcement concerning the Canadian New Housing Price Index. In order to avoid trading too close to the news announcement time and any possible extreme price reaction against my trade, Trade 1 was closed early at 1.6942 for 18 pips.

The price reaction to the news was not as volatile as I had anticipated but cautionary measures like exiting a trade prevents traders from being trapped in an unusually big price move in the wrong direction.

This early exit meant it was time to consider double dipping.

After price settled, I looked for another opportunity to continue trading the downtrend. It is not a simple matter of a random click and enter if you plan on going for the second dip. We should go back to the original trading plan and find another trade consistent with our entry criteria.

Using the same criteria as before for Trade 1, we look for an entry point to open Trade 2. The 10R chart remained the same with the downtrend still strongly supported by the short-term GMMA and the long-term GMMA. On the 3R chart, another opportunity presented itself when the short-term GMMA compressed around the area marked by the down arrow at Trade 2. The probability of price breaking out and down again was high given the wider downtrend seen on the 10R chart.

A short position, Trade 2 was opened at 1.6921 as marked on the 3R chart with a Profit Target at 1.6821 and a Stop Loss at 1.6945. For Trade 2, a new Profit Target was calculated according to the Support and Resistance lines on a 1-hour chart and the new initial Stop Loss was calculated according to the Traders ATR line on the 10R chart. The target price was achieved at 1.6821 for 100 pips. Together, Trade 1 and Trade 2 yielded a total of 118 pips. We took an 18-pip bite but returned successfully for an additional 100-pip double dip.

Double dipping in trading is possible where the trading plan criteria is consistently applied to every potential new trade. Despite already having taken a bite, going in for the second dip is definitely worth it when the second dip is consistent with the initial trade plan. It sounds good on paper, but sometimes what you see is not what you get, so how to recognise and manage this "black hole" risk?

Placing an order for a Take Profit target usually rests on the assumption the order is filled if the set price is reached. I questioned this assumption after the completion of one of my FX trades in GBPAUD. Despite having reached the desired price level, the action of price itself did not trigger the Take Profit order to close out my trade. I wanted to investigate this mysterious disappearance of price into what appeared to be a "black hole" on my chart because, left unexplained, this has the potential to wreck the best laid trading plans.

The following GBPAUD trade became the mystery trade I needed to solve. First step was to examine the trade strategy for any analysis flaws. Using the ANTSSYS 321 strategy, I used three range bar charts: 7R for the general trend direction, 5R for the confirmation of trend, and 3R for the entry chart.

On the 7R long-term directional chart, Figure 8.3, the overall downward trend is clear. The short-term GMMA lines sitting below the long-term GMMA lines are well separated, showing strong support for the continuation of the trend in the downwards direction. The order of the short-term GMMA below the long-term GMMA confirms the definite downtrend in place. The 3R chart confirmed the analysis. The strategy

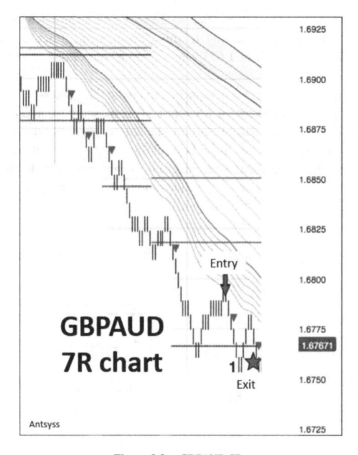

**Figure 8.3.** GBPAUD 7R.

seemed sound so the black hole in this trade was potentially located elsewhere so I followed the market action.

Price began to move down, and upon the opening of the Frankfurt Forex Market, an extreme price movement completed in a matter of milliseconds saw price rapidly reach my target profit. My elation turned to confusion as my trade was still showing as an open trade yet I could see price had moved beyond my Take Profit order.

It's a basic rule of the market. If your sell order is at $100 and the market completed trades at $101, then this means ALL sell orders below $101 must have been filled before the next sale at $101 takes place.

A second opportunity for price to go to target occurred when price moved back up before turning to trend down again. Price eventually reached my Take Profit of 1.6757 and my trade was closed at a profit of 27 pips.

The big question was what happened to create this "black hole"? Why wasn't my sell order executed when price first moved beyond that level? It is a big question because we need to be able to get out at the price we specify when traded prices move beyond this level. If our sell orders are ignored by the market then we need to adjust strategies accordingly.

An email sent to my broker provided me with an answer. Figure 8.4's chart demonstrates what had happened.

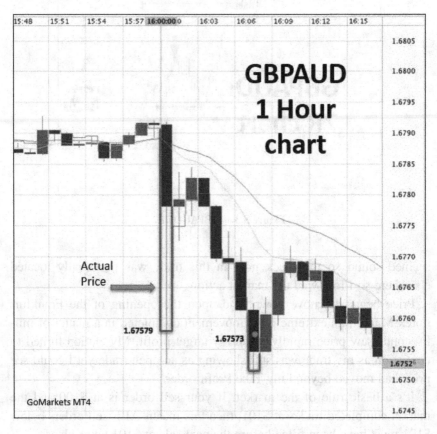

**Figure 8.4.** GBPAUD 1-hour chart.

It was quite simple. At the Frankfurt market opening at 16:00, the long shadow tail under the long candle reached a low of 1.6752. This was 5 pips beyond my Take Profit target of 1.6757. The FX platform I use calculates the candlestick chart based on *average* prices. This is the chart I refer to for analysis and monitoring during trading. When I overlayed the *actual* ask price indicator as seen by the outline around the long shadow tail, I saw how my price was not actually met. The line under the long candle at 16:00 showed the actual low ask price to be 1.67579. My Take Profit price order, shown above as the dot at 16:06, was 1.67573. To be exact, I was 0.00006 of a pip short.

Extreme volatility results in price not being met for many reasons. In this particular situation, the answer was found not on the range-based ANTS chart but within the FX platform itself.

Here is the critical difference. *Average* price was used to create the chart and *actual* price was used to fill the trade orders. Check with your broker in order to avoid black holes. What you see is not always what you get.

Double dip trading in a good trend works for as long as the trend continues. The uncertainty lies in the timing of the entry into a trend. Entering the trend early or entering the trend after it has had time to establish are decisions every trader must consider.

# Chapter 9

# Rise of the Mid-trend Trade

Many traders believe the trend is your friend. Like any good friendship and any good trend, where it might end is anyone's guess. Taking a trade at the very beginning of a trend on the assumption it will take off is a high-risk activity but it offers the maximum profit potential. Waiting to enter a trend after it has had some time to establish itself increases your probability of achieving your Profit Target but reduces your overall profit. Managing these conflicting expectations is a challenge for all traders. Go for the large profit or go for safety and a smaller profit?

Let's examine an example of what I categorise as a mid-trend trade where price is already trending together with the short-term GMMA and the long-term GMMA moving in one direction. This trade comes from EURAUD.

For this ANTSSYS 321 trade I use three range bar charts. A 7R for the general trend direction, 5R for the confirmation of trend, and 3R for the Entry chart.

On the 5R confirmation chart, Figure 9.1, EURAUD was clearly trending upwards. The short-term GMMA lines were above the long-term GMMA lines in the correct order for an uptrend. The 7R direction chart looked almost identical.

The trend was well established so the question becomes, is there enough profit left to make the trade worthwhile?

The ANTSSYS method uses the concept of an 85% probability for achieving 75% of the 5-day Average Daily Range (ADR) value. This concept is explained in more detail in Chapter 22. For this discussion, we just need to know the trade target is at 1.5102. On the 3R chart, Figure 9.2, the entry to the trade is below the 50% line. As price has an 85% probability

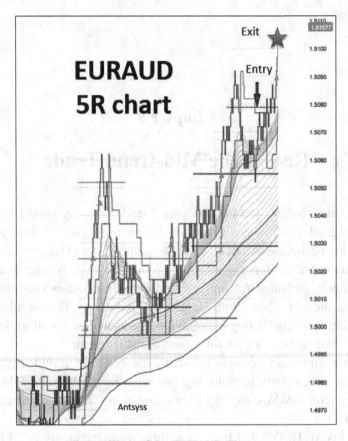

**Figure 9.1.** EURAUD 5R.

of reaching the 75% line, we know a Target Profit set at any price up to this line is achievable. Any Target Profit set above the 75% line becomes lower in probability. If the intention is to continue to make more profit after this level then we need to exercise caution knowing there may not be much more profit to be made in the trade.

On the 3R chart, Figure 9.2, price had moved upwards and was in an established uptrend. The short-term GMMA lines compressed around the area marked by the down arrow. This signals an upcoming price change either up or down. From the 5R chart, Figure 9.1, we know the established trend is up. Based on the strength of trend evidence on the 7R and 5R

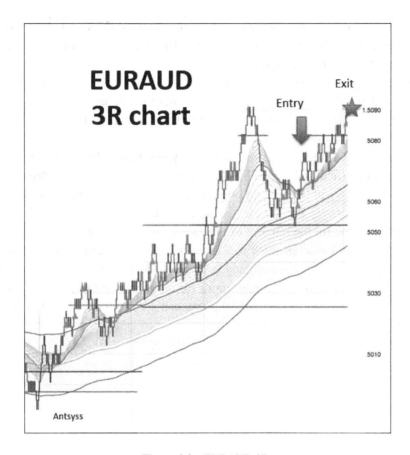

**Figure 9.2**   EURAUD 3R.

charts, there was a high probability of price breaking out of the compression to continue up. A short-term trade was opened with an entry made at 1.5072, a Stop Loss at 1.4042, and a Take Profit target at 1.5102.

Price steadily moved up and the short-term GMMA started to expand up in line with the uptrend. There was a sudden surge in price momentum and the trade was closed at 1.5102. A profit of 30 pips.

This mid-trend entry paid off because:

(1) The compression of the short-term GMMA on the 3R Entry chart was an indication of a pause in the trend before the price broke out to continue the uptrend.

(2) The confirmation chart where the long-term GMMA and short-term GMMA indicated the trend remained strong, the probability of the continuing trend was high.

(3) There was more than one reason for the trend to continue. The more evidence found on the charts, the higher the probability for price to continue to move in our desired direction and for further profit.

If these conditions are met then it may not be too late to enter mid-trend. It is difficult to predict how much more profit can be extracted from a continuing trend because no one knows when the trend will come to an end. However, we can assess the trend against our preferred indicator conditions and tip the balance of probability in our favour.

This doesn't always work and sometimes we get out too early. What should we do if we have already exited a trade only to see signals of a continuing trend with the opportunity for potentially more profit? That's the issue addressed in Chapter 10 because it's a different type of double dipping.

# Chapter 10

# The Long and the Short of It

Prices trend up or down in every market. Within the bigger picture trend there are also smaller trends to be found. A strategy to trade with the overall general trend is the standard approach but it is also possible to trade against it, long or short. This is called fading the trend. There are many opportunities to trade these inner trends on an intraday basis using shorter time frames or smaller range bar charts. This switching from a long-side to a short-side trade is also associated with a Stop and Reverse strategies. This should not be confused with the SAR indicator. How you trade depends on the price action at the time.

The following trade on the USDJPY illustrates the strategy. It is based on the ANTSSYS 321 strategy and shifts from short-side to long-side trades within the prevailing long-term trend. For this trade I used only two range bar charts: 5R for the general direction and 3R for the entry chart.

The reason for choosing a lower timeframe 5R chart, Figure 10.1, as the directional chart is because the Average Daily Range (ADR) value was low at only 75. The ADR provides a guideline of the potential range of price for the current day's activity. The calculation and application are discussed in Chapter 22. For this discussion we only need to know that the ADR number is used as a guide in determining the potential number of pips a currency pair may move in a day.

There is an 85% probability of achieving 75% of the 5-day ADR value. Of course, the higher the ADR number, the higher the potential for the currency to move. With low ADR values, tightening of the ranges of the bars in the ANTS 321 strategy gives a better picture of the current price action.

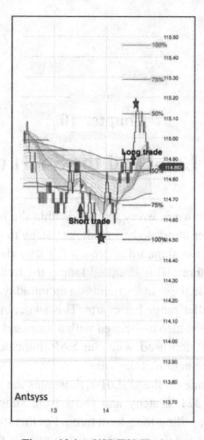

**Figure 10.1.** USDJPY 5R chart.

On the 5R chart, the area labeled "Short trade" is where the short-term GMMA lines have compressed and are sitting below the long-term GMMA indicating the overall trend as down. Looking at the area labelled "Long trade", the short-term GMMA has already compressed and expanded, making a decisive move up through the long-term GMMA. When the short-term GMMA moves up to position itself above the long-term GMMA, it is in the correct order for an uptrend. The trend is changing from a downtrend and beginning to change to an uptrend. This is an opportunity to open a trade on the long side.

Given the correct signals, it is possible to look for short-trade as well as long-trade opportunities on the same chart.

**Figure 10.2.** Entry signals USDJPY 3R chart.

The first trade opportunity on the 3R chart, Figure 10.2, was a short trade entered into at 114.68 with a Take Profit target of 114.40 and a Stop Loss of 114.85.

Initially the move on this trade saw price move down past 114.55. Price moved down to touch this level a few times, proving to be a strong level of resistance, suggesting the trade would not meet its full potential. A decision was made to close the short trade at 114.55 for 13 pips.

The next opportunity on the 3R chart presented itself in the form of a long trade. A long trade was entered into at 114.97 with a Take Profit target of 115.20 and Stop Loss of 114.74.

Price moved rapidly up. A number of times price stopped at 115.12. This became a level of resistance. Unable to push through this resistance level several times, it finally made a breakthrough up to the 115.17 level but only briefly. At 115.17, it was 3 pips short of my Take Profit target. As price retraced, the trade was closed at 115.11 for 14 pips.

The long and the short of this USDJPY trade example is the potential of one chart to identify two different opportunities. Both were monitored using careful trade management and each one resulted in a profit. We have the choice to fade the trend or apply Stop and Reverse strategies to maximise opportunities.

Every trade is different. Depending on the way the trade is managed, the profit result is also different. In Chapter 11, we look at trade management in more detail to see various methods of profit maximisation.

# Chapter 11

# Three Trade Bites Make Up a Whole

A Chinese tea drinking tradition is *san kou*, or three mouthfuls to empty the tea cup. Some traders offer the same opportunity to take three, in this case, bites out of a trade.

Taking a trade exit is not always easy. Sometimes the exit is too early and the trend continues after a minor stumble. At other times the problem is amplified because the market has hurt us with a series of losses. This saps confidence, and we get out of trades just to take a small profit rather than run the risk of them turning into a loss. It is important to overcome this loss of confidence to improve in our trading.

Following a string of bad trades there is a natural tendency to become overcautious and develop what we might call a nervous "traders twitch". The following trades illustrate how I worked with the ANTSSYS 321 strategy to overcome this traders twitch and get back into the trend.

On the right side of the 10R chart, Figure 11.1, the short-term GMMA had earlier compressed, turned, and was passing down through the long-term GMMA. With the short-term GMMA lines sitting below the long-term GMMA lines, there is a definite downtrend in place. This is a great trading environment for short-side trades, if only I could overcome the traders twitch.

On the 3R chart, Figure 11.2, the short-term GMMA has compressed and is also at the early beginnings of a move down as marked by the first up arrow.

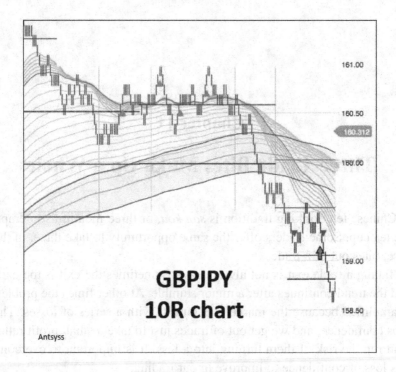

**Figure 11.1.**   GBPJPY 10R.

## Initial Trade Bite #1

Ideally, the point of preferred entry is at the beginning of the trend. At the time of compression of the short-term GMMA on the 3R chart, it is difficult to make a call on price direction. Some traders are willing to make the call early while other traders wait for further confirmation of the direction of the move. Sometimes we miss optimal entries when we can't be at our computer at the right time. At the first up arrow, Trade bite #1, the lines of the short-term GMMA have only just begun to separate out slightly in a down direction. Referring back to the 10R chart, Figure 11.1, we can clearly see a definite overall direction of a downtrend. The early compression seen on the 3R chart was highly likely to break out and downwards.

Confident of a further downward price movement, a short trade was entered into at 159.28 with a Stop Loss at 159.38 for 10 pips and a Take

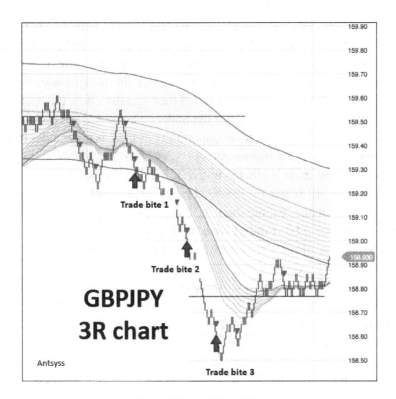

**Figure 11.2.** GBPJPY 3R.

Profit target at 158.98 for 30 pips. As the trade moved into profit then retraced, I twitched and exited the trade quickly in order to preserve my profits. The last thing I wanted was to make another loss to add to my previous string of small losses. Price retraced back to the original entry price. My twitchy exit only yielded 8 pips of profit.

Time, like Lady Macbeth said, to screw my courage to the sticking place. Trading cannot be ruled by a twitch.

## Trade Bite #2

After the small retracement, price resumed its downward direction. The first step is to calmly re-analyse the trend and price behaviour. We have to convince ourselves the trade is justifiable. From the area before the second up arrow on the 3R chart, the moving average lines of both the short-term GMMA and the long-term GMMA were well separated and looking very supportive of the developing downwards movement. The downtrend emerging is more obvious than at the time of the initial trade. For the trader who prefers more confirmation of the trend direction, this would be a good place for a trade entry. For the traders who closed the trade a little prematurely, this is another trade opportunity as there is potentially further downtrend to this price movement.

Another short trade is entered into at 159.13 with a Stop Loss at 159.23 and a Take Profit target of 158.53. Price fails to reach over 20 pips so I twitched again and exit the trade at 15 pips. In hindsight it doesn't make sense to exit again but I didn't have my usual confidence to ride through the rollercoaster of price movements. Emotions were overriding my trade plan.

Perhaps if this was a trade after a string of good trades I would have been more confident and willing to tolerate wider price retracements to keep me in the trade for longer. Your mind is a powerful tool in trading. It works with you or it works against you.

Time to again screw my courage to the sticking place. It's not easy to do after a string of losses, but it is essential to eliminate the traders twitch.

## Trade Bite #3

Again we need to buckle down and clearly analyse the chart and the trend behaviour. If this was an entirely new trade I had just come across, would I take it? If yes, then we take it as a third trade in this series.

At the third up arrow on the 3R chart, the short-term GMMA and the long-term GMMA moving averages were widening again slightly, offering a further sign of momentum in the downward movement. Another new short-side trade is opened. The Take Profit target was set at 10 pips. This target price level was achieved and the profit secured.

From the initial entry at 159.28 to the lowest point at 158.50 there was the potential for a total of 78 pips. The traders twitch made achieving even lower levels of profit difficult because of the multiple entries. Developing the confidence to enter mid-trend trades, or re-enter mid-trend trades, is an important skill in obtaining steady profits from trading.

What do we learn from this exercise? Each additional trade entered into is assessed as a completely new trade. After the completion of these three bite-sized trades, the downward momentum was broken and price retraced back into the long-term GMMA group. With a total of 33 pips, the ANTSSYS 321 goal of taking profit of 30 pips was achieved. With it I also beat the twitch and regained some of my confidence ready in time for the next trade.

Taking two or more bites out of the trade should not be confused with revenge trading or chasing losses. All traders were entered after the previous trade had been closed at a profit.

After an exit from a trade, there are times when the signals on the chart indicate a trend change. Chapter 12 shows how it is possible to be trading long for one trade then short for another trade with both trades generating profits. This is sometimes called stop and reverse trading.

# Chapter 12

# Trade Management — A Comparison of Three Ways to Profit

Choosing a real estate agent to sell your house is a hard decision. Each agent has a strategy to get you the best price but the big question is who has the ability to get you the highest price so you get the highest profit. In trading there are also many ways to manage a trade. When the trade is in profit — in the money — the hard decision is how to manage and maximise this profit. We look at three ways of managing profit and compare each result. This analysis of profit optimisation is a useful exercise but it should never become a distraction. We always aim for the best profit available in the circumstances rather than the best possible profit.

Here's the overview of the trade — entry to exit — we use as a base to evaluate three exit methods. Using the ANTSSYS 321 strategy, the goal for a trade is 30 pips. In this EURCAD trade, a 7R chart is used for the long-term direction, a 5R chart for medium-term confirmation, and a 3R chart for the entry chart.

On the 7R chart, the short-term GMMA lines had compressed and started to turn down passing through the long-term GMMA group. The trend is beginning to turn down.

Starting from the left side of the 3R chart, Figure 12.1, both the short-term GMMA and the long-term GMMA have already compressed and turned over, heading in the downwards direction.

A short trade was entered into at 1.4760. The trade moved into profit and quickly reached the 30-pip Target Profit of 1.4730. The well-separated lines of the short-term GMMA and the long-term GMMA indicated

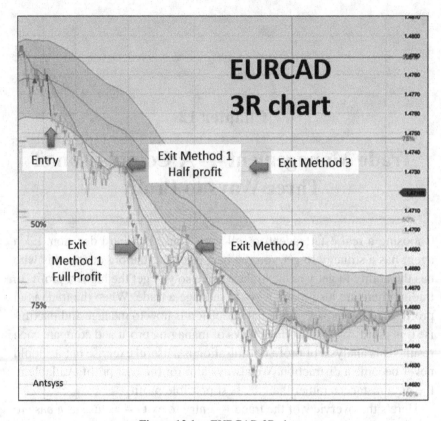

**Figure 12.1.** EURCAD 3R chart.

strong support of a downwards trend with the potential to last much longer than the targeted 30 pips.

## Following the Trade Closely to Maximise Profits

In order to follow the bigger move for longer, I scaled out half of the position at 1.4730 and let the remaining half run. The 50% and 75% ADR levels of EURCAD are calculated and marked on the 3R chart. As explained in Chapter 22, there is an 85% probability of achieving 75% of the 5-day ADR value. Based on the knowledge of this probability, reaching the 50% ADR level is achievable. After taking 30 pips of profit, my new Take Profit target level was moved to the 50% ADR level. As price passed this point, a new Take Profit level was set halfway between the 50% line and 75% line. A trailing Stop Loss of 20 pips from the current price served to preserve accumulating profits as well as to allow some fluctuations in price movements without getting stopped out too prematurely.

Confidence grew with the anticipation of profits running past the 100% line. I was quickly brought back to reality when stopped out at 1.4690. The resulting profit was an additional 40-pip movement to the original Take Profit target of 30 pips.

## Alternative Trade Management Methods

Could I have done better? This is a little like worrying about a sore tooth, but this analysis is useful to improve the way we manage our trades.

Table 12.1 compares the different trade management methods and reveals the one for maximising profit.

From the comparison table, Method 2 was the winner in terms of maximising profit for this particular short trade on the EURCAD. It was marginally better than Method 3 if we had chosen a Take Profit at a predetermined 60 pips. Method 1 of closing half the trade and letting the remaining position run was the least preferred method for this trade.

**Table 12.1.**  Trade management comparison based on 80,000 units.

EURCAD

| | Entry | Profit Target | Pips | Pip Value | Profit | |
|---|---|---|---|---|---|---|
| **Method 1** Close half the trade first then let remaining profitable units run | 1.4760 | 1.4730 | 30 | 8.32 | | |
| | 1.4760 | 1.4690 | 70 | 8.32 | $ 416.00 | *** |
| **Method 2** Take profit when trade ends | 1.4760 | 1.4690 | 70 | 8.32 | $ 582.40 | |
| **Method 3** Take profit at a predetermined (60) pip target | 1.4760 | 1.4700 | 60 | 8.32 | $ 499.20 | |

***Profit calculation is divided by 2 to account for both half positions

## Best Trade Management Method

In managing a profitable trade, choose the trade management style most suitable to your temperament.

**Method 1** — Close half the trade first and then let the remaining profitable
units run
This is suitable for the trader who likes some security in locking in some profit along the way.

**Method 2** — Take Profit when the trade ends
This is for the trader who doesn't mind the extended risk associated with letting profits run. Maximum profit is the best outcome of this method if the trader chooses the right time to exit the trade. There is also the possibility of giving some profit back if it is not the best exit.

**Method 3** — Take Profit at a predetermined (60) pip target
This is for the goal oriented trader who is disciplined enough to close a trade when it gets to target and would be satisfied with the resulting profit regardless of whether or not the trade has the capacity to generate more profit.

Although my chosen method resulted in the least favourable outcome for this trade, I have no complaints as it was the correct one in terms of my approach to trading. I am comfortable with locking in some profit after a trade becomes profitable and adding to what is already in the bank if there is more profit to come. Besides, one never regrets a profit.

Profit may be growing steadily for a trader along with the overall trend but significant events beyond our control have the capacity to affect the price. In equity trading, the Share Purchase Plan announcements are one of these events, so we look at how to manage such events while adhering to the rules of our trading plan.

# Chapter 13

# Tale of a GUD Trade Gone Bad

A sudden windfall profit rewards you beyond your expected trade target or a share price plummets for no apparent reason. For good trade management, we must anticipate how to react in these situations. At the very least, it should be written into our trading plan. We need to consider the decisions required in response to such circumstances. Capturing an unexpected profit or cutting an unexpected loss has a significant impact on our aggregate trading results. Often these outliers of performance contribute substantially to enhance or destroy our trading.

This trade in GUD captures both the consequences of both a profit boost and a damaging sudden loss. How this happened is not important. This example illustrates the consequences of not planning for the unusual and provides a solution.

Eyeballing the Weekly charts of the index stocks, GUD Holdings (GUD), Figure 13.1, stood out as it showed a good long-term GMMA with widely spaced lines indicating a slow steady rise in share price. The short-term GMMAs sitting above the long-term group were well separated and moving in an uptrend.

Compression of the short-term GMMA around the area of our entry as marked on the Daily chart, Figure 13.2, signalled an agreement in price and the potential for price to breakout. Against the background of the uptrend showing on the Weekly chart, the probability of the breakout was most likely up. A trade on GUD was opened at an entry price of $7.77, with a profit target set at $8.54 and an ATR Stop Loss set at $7.40 for initial capital preservation in case the trade failed.

GUD was in loss for a few days before becoming profitable. GUD's share price continued to rise with a one day spike of 8%. My profit target

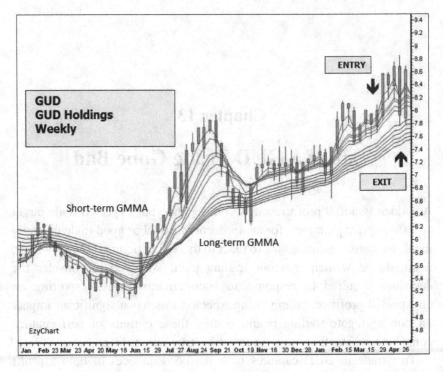

GUD
GUD Holdings
Weekly

ENTRY

EXIT

Short-term GMMA

Long-term GMMA

EzyChart

Jan  Feb 23 Mar 23 Apr 20 May 18 Jun 15  29 Jul 27 Aug 24 Sep 21 Oct 19 Nov 16  30 Dec 28 Jan  Feb 15 Mar 15  29 Apr 26

**Figure 13.1.** Using long-term GMMA for trend strength.

of $8.54 was met on intraday prices. Unfortunately I missed the opportunity to sell at the target price. An intraday spike straight to the target price was not a scenario I had factored in. The scenario I had imagined saw price reaching the target price by the close of trade then over the next day I would calmly place an order on the open to claim my easy profit.

Our trade does not always follow our imagination or our dreams in such an ordered fashion. I missed the chance to sell because I wasn't at the computer at the right time to click the sell button. Most importantly, I didn't have a sell order in place to capture the profit at the exact moment. After the price spike, price began to retreat from the highs of the day. At this point I had to make a decision. Sell to lock in a lower profit or preserve the remains of the windfall gain in anticipation of price rises to come. Indecision led to the default position so I continued to hold GUD (Figure 13.2).

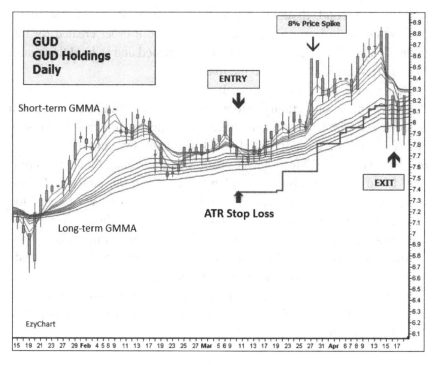

**Figure 13.2.** Consequences of indecision.

Luck is a fortune, but it is potentially a fortune lost as well as a fortune won. In this case it was, at first, a fortune won. This encourages ill-discipline because indecision is rewarded. GUD's price continued upwards, fuelling my belief of further increases in the share price. The clear blue skies ahead turned grey very quickly. On the 13th day after the initial upwards price spike, price suddenly spiked downwards around 10% reaching an intraday low of $7.77, equal to the original entry price!

A trailing protect profit order is an order placed with your broker to sell at a predetermined price if the stock reaches a trigger price. It saves us time sitting at the computer knowing profit is immediately captured as soon as price reaches its target whether it is intraday or end of day. We have the ability to set and forget.

When price does reach the target, all emotions are removed from the sell process. The decision to sell has been made and the sell executes without a second thought. There is no hope or greed for more. Unfortunately there wasn't a trailing protect profit order created for this trade. I had expected the price target to be reached and to hold there until I had placed my sell order into the market.

Opportunity has a use-by date. It's there and then it's not, it expires. Best to act on an opportunity before it disappears. A trailing protect profit order placed with a broker would have automatically triggered on intraday prices and locked in my profit at $8.54 per share. Instead GUD was sold the next day at $8.04 for a lower profit. My immediate thoughts were if only I had followed my trading plan to sell when the target profit was achieved or if only I had created a protect profit order. Two actions, too simple. Either would have saved the trade and the disappointment of watching profit erode away to around a third of what it once was.

Markets are unpredictable and volatile. Consideration should be made to protect against sudden price moves if possible. Creating a protect profit order immediately after entering a trade is one suggested option. Write this into your trading plan if this suits and implement it. Don't let a "GUD" trade turn bad.

# Part 2

# Wrestling with Risk

# Chapter 14

# Defend Your Position

Italy in 2006, Spain in 2010, and Germany in 2014. All were FIFA World Cup one-time champions with no repeat performances since their tournament wins. In 2018, Italy didn't even get a spot in the World Cup group stage while Germany and Spain were eliminated in the first round. Maybe these teams relied on the same "winning" strategies while their opponents improved. Likewise in trading, the same strategy from four years or even four days ago might not work today. Markets change and we need to adapt our trading to suit the environment we trade in.

Does this sound familiar to you? After a run of successful trades you are stopped out too early in some trades. To your chagrin, price then turns around and achieves the target profit you had originally set. Is this a change in the market condition, or a fault in the way you set stops?

When this happened to me, then careful examination suggested the fault was with the way I set my stops. They were mathematically correct, but in practice not so useful. After being stopped out of trades that go on to be successful, some traders decide to stop using stops. It works for a short time until they go broke because using no stop is a fast path to disaster. The better solution is to re-examine how I was using stops.

Thinking outside the box made me realise it is possible to put a Stop Loss where it *should* be and not just where I want it to be based on a calculation formula. The following FX trade on the EURJPY demonstrates what it means to adapt to the environment of the trade. Guppy talks of this as placing a stop at logical chart-based points and then adjusting trade size to reach the desired risk management targets.

As an intraday FX trader, one of the Forex trading methods I use is based on a Price Action Strategy. This method was introduced in

Chapter 8. It's a method used to set a better Stop Loss point as shown in this EURJPY example.

Using a top down multiple time frame analysis, the starting point for this trade is the 4-hour chart, Figure 14.1. Price hits the support line several times at 127.79, forming a triple bottom. There is potential for the EURJPY price to move up from this price area. The next step is to look at another smaller timeframe to investigate the action of price further to see if the position of this pause point is confirmed. We shift from a 4-hour chart to a 1-hour chart.

A double bottom is seen on the EURJPY 1-hour chart, Figure 14.2, as indicated by the two horizontal lines. This is added confirmation of price wanting to move up. A trendline is drawn and we focus on this, looking for price to break. In order to get closer to what price is doing, we look to the next timeframe down for an entry, using a 15-minute chart.

The 15-minute chart, Figure 14.3, is used as the trade Entry chart. Price has broken through the inner trendline with a back end retest of the line. It is on the retest we have the signal for an entry. A long trade is opened

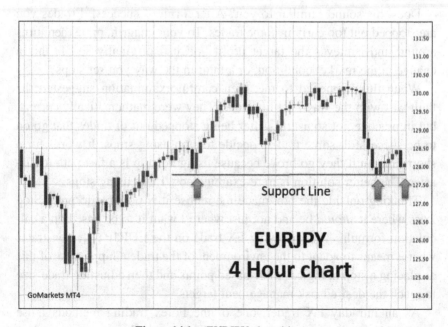

**Figure 14.1.**   EURJPY chart 4 hour.

**Figure 14.2.** EURJPY chart 1 hour.

on the EURJPY with an entry price of 128.11, a Stop Loss of 127.93, and a Take Profit price of 128.27.

For short-term FX trading I am not keen on anything larger than a 20-pip Stop Loss as this isn't a comfortable risk for my account. On opening the trade some slippage occurred resulting in a risk of 18 pips to a reward of 16 pips. This is acceptable to me as a close enough 1:1 ratio for this trade. At the time, the more logical Stop Loss placement was below the last low at around the price of 127.83. A Stop Loss of 28 pips from the entry price of 128.11. Since I knew I couldn't "afford" it as the risk was too high compared to the reward, I left the original Stop Loss in the market at 127.93 for 18 pips.

If a risk of 28 pips at the logical Stop Loss would result in an undesirable substantial loss on your capital, then reducing the position size is a possible solution. For example, a position size on GBPAUD of 500,000 units equates to $50 per pip. At 28 pips × $50 it is a potential loss of $1,400. The damage of this loss on an account balance of $15,000 would be equal to 9% of trading capital. This is a trade we can't "afford". By

**Figure 14.3.** EURJPY Entry chart 15 minute.

reducing the position size of the trade we make this trade into one we are able to "afford". Instead of 500,000 units, a reduced position size to 100,000 units changes the value per pip to $10. At 28 pips × $10 it is a potential loss of $280. On an account balance of $15,000, the loss would be equal to 2% of trading capital. By taking trades like this where risk is a small percentage of our capital, we stay in business for longer. The other side of the equation is the reward, the target profit. This is up to individuals to calculate and identify possible logical profit targets.

Figure 14.4's chart shows how the trade developed.

Price rose and was in profit until the high marked by the star. Then price turned and continued lower, triggering the Stop Loss at 127.93 as seen on the chart at the side arrow. If I had used a logical Stop Loss at 127.83 then price would have had the room to move down before moving

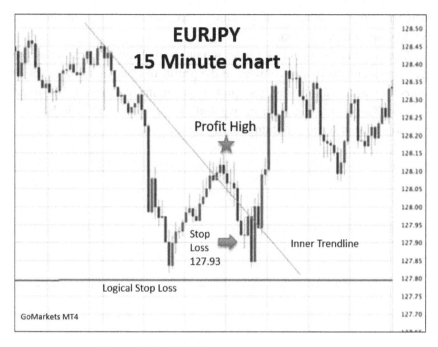

**Figure 14.4.** EURJPY post-trade chart 15 minute.

up again and achieving the original price target of 128.27. In this trade, the stop was too tight and resulted in an unnecessary early exit.

The problem created by using the same standard strategy of setting "X" number of pips for each trade regardless of where the Stop Loss should have been led to the Stop Loss being triggered and closed prematurely in terms of its trend behaviour.

There are two possible solutions in this situation.

1. Don't take the trade. The cost of a potential loss is too expensive.
2. Take the trade but reduce the position size. This reduces the dollar per pip and makes the trade more "affordable".

Setting the Stop Loss in a logical place keeps us in a trade for longer. Constantly working on the areas of your strategy requiring improvement increases your probability of yielding more winners. Look to the next World Cup, not the last one.

Once we survive the initial phase and our trade becomes profitable, the next consideration is how to manage the profit. In Chapter 15, we look at protecting and maximising our profits given the uncertainty of trend duration. Once a trade is in profit we don't want to lose any of it, but neither do we want to miss out on making more.

# Chapter 15

# Milking the Trade

One cow is milked for 30 litres of milk on average per day. It is only an average. Sometimes the cow gives less, sometimes more. One trade has the potential to be profitable for a number of traders and depending on the trader, some get more profit out of the trade, others less. Depending on the strategy for managing the trade to maximise the profit, the results invariably differ.

We use an A2 Milk (A2M) Company trade to examine how different strategies deliver different results depending on the trade management method applied.

When on the hunt for a good trade, I like to scan for stocks trending well both on the Daily and the Weekly charts. The A2M Company met both these prerequisites for opening a trade. GMMAs together with price action make a good combination for selecting a good trend. The A2M charts passed the initial eyeball test with both the short-term GMMA and the long-term GMMA showing good support of the uptrend in progress.

The A2M Company Weekly chart, Figure 15.1, shows a good separation of the short-term GMMA lines and the long-term GMMA lines. It is a good indication for the uptrend to most likely continue.

How long is this trend likely to continue for? Is an imminent collapse of the trend due after I enter the trade? Or does the trend still have a long run ahead? It is an accepted part of trading to never know these answers with certainty. The next chart shows my trade management of the stock as price began to move into profit. For many traders, this is one of the most difficult aspects of trading. This is a solution I use.

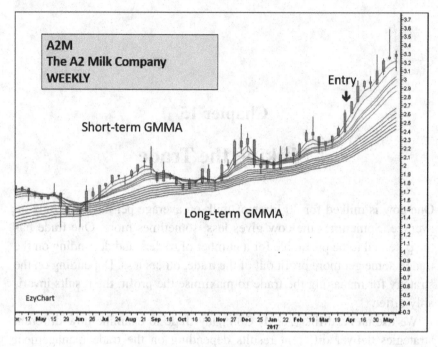

**Figure 15.1.** A2M Weekly chart.

The A2M Daily chart, Figure 15.2, showed the same short-term and long-term GMMA characteristics as the Weekly chart. Good separation of the lines were indicative of strong support for the uptrend taking place. The trade was entered into at $2.64. The initial Stop Loss for the trade was $2.46 and the Target Profit exit price was $3.02.

A 2*ATR Stop Loss was marked under price. As price moved up and the trade became profitable, the ATR Stop Loss moved up with it, becoming our trailing Stop Loss. We want to keep our profits while lowering our risk of a loss. I used a Falling Sell Order at the initial Stop Loss of $2.46 to protect my trade.

When price reached the Target Profit, I wanted to let profits run so I kept a close watch on price and my Stop Loss. Price continued up and I changed my Stop Loss the next day to the most current 2*ATR Stop Loss value of $3.14. On this day, the high price was $3.54. This was above my

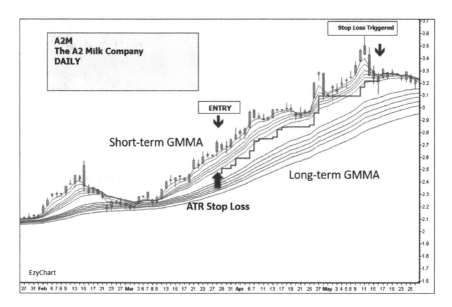

**Figure 15.2.**   A2M Daily chart.

original Planned Profit exit target of \$3.02. Price peaked, as did my greed. Price retreated, but my greed did not so the trade remained open. A few days later, my Falling Sell Order was triggered intraday at \$3.14 and the trade was closed.

An interesting post-trade question based on Stop Loss strategies is how much could another trader have "milked" from this trade by utilising and managing the ATR Stop Loss in different ways.

It's a little like probing a sore tooth, but examining better exit solutions improves the way you capture trading profits. It's not about regret. It's about learning and improving.

If Trader 1 (T1) used the 2*ATR Stop Loss, the trade was closed out as marked T1 on the chart in Figure 15.3. This strategy results in a profit of **\$0.45** or 17%.

If Trader 2 (T2) used a 1*ATR Stop Loss, the trade closed out on the same day as Trader 1 but at a higher price of \$3.15. This strategy delivers a profit of **\$0.51** or 19%.

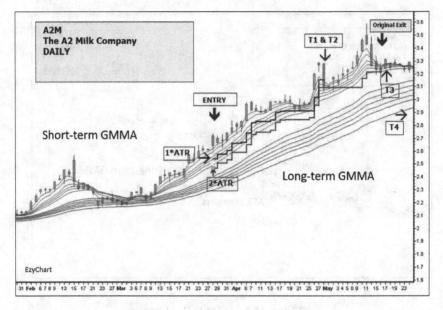

**Figure 15.3.** A2M trade development.

If Trader 3 (T3) used End of Day price for their 2*ATR Stop Loss, they would not have had to close the trade on the same day as Trader 1 and Trader 2. Over the next two days, the closing prices were above the 2*ATR Stop Loss level, keeping Trader 3 in the trade. The trade closed as marked T3, the day after price closed on the 2*ATR line to yield a profit of **$0.57** per share or 22%.

The final strategy is where Trader 4 (T4) uses an End of Day price for their 2*ATR Stop Loss and waits for a close below the 2*ATR Stop Loss line. In this strategy, they remain in the trade at $3.27 for an unrealised profit of **$0.63** per share or 24%.

At the peak of the trade, A2M hit $3.54 and I was sitting on an unrealised profit of **$0.90** per share. A 37% return. So what did I "milk" out of this A2M share trade? I took a profit of **$0.50** per share, representing a return of 19% over a 49-day period. For me, it is better to have a disciplined exit on a Stop Loss because this consistently protects against the risk of trend collapse.

The best strategy for maximising profit differs for each individual trade. The question of whether we have extracted the maximum profit from a trade is answered only after the trade is closed. Finding a good strategy to consistently capture an average return from each trade is realistic and achievable. If you wish to improve on your strategy to extract more profit from future trades, acknowledging the extra effort does not necessarily equate to extra reward.

There are no guarantees of trend continuation for any trade taken, though we should at least manage our trade once we are in profit. The next step is figuring out the best time to take a profit. It is the ultimate question.

# Chapter 16

# The Ultimate Question

During the Vietnam War, Jeff Stein, a US Army Intelligence Officer, controlled a network of Vietnamese spies. His rival during that time was General Tran Tien Cung who ran agents against him. Fifty years after the war, Stein made the journey back to Vietnam to finally meet Cung who was now very frail having suffered a stroke. Unanswered questions had accumulated in his head over the years but Stein was only permitted to ask one. After much thought and consideration he finally spoke and asked, "What was your greatest espionage triumph against us?"

We are not in the same situation, but this type of ultimate question helps focus our analysis. Out of the many questions we may have about capturing a successful trade, if we could only ask one, what would that question be?

For me the one question to ask would be about the best way to manage a trade. If only I knew exactly when to close a trade to maximise profits. Or when to close a trade to minimise losses and know price will not then suddenly turn around to travel in my preferred direction again. In a world of perfect market information, I might not even open a trade knowing it wouldn't be a profitable one.

Such a risk-free environment doesn't exist. The following EURNZD trade demonstrates one trade management method of capturing some profit when there is an uncertainty about whether price will be able to reach a calculated target. It is based on the ANTSSYS 321 strategy.

This EURNZD trade uses the 7R chart for the general trend direction and the 3R chart for the entry.

On the 7R long-term directional chart, Figure 16.1, the overall trend is up. The short-term GMMA lines and the long-term GMMA lines are well separated, showing support for the continuation of the trend.

On the 3R chart, Figure 16.2, leading up to the marked entry point, the short-term GMMAs have turned, crossed upwards, and sit above the long-term GMMA. An uptrend is in place and confirmed with the direction of the 7R chart.

A long trade on EURNZD is entered at 1.6480 as marked by the up arrow in Figure 16.2. The Stop Loss is 1.6452 as marked on the 5R chart, Figure 16.2, and the Take Profit is set at 1.6510.

The ultimate question of knowing the exact time to close a trade for maximum profit cannot be answered without a crystal ball. It is a question with no ultimate definitive answer. When we realise this, the most

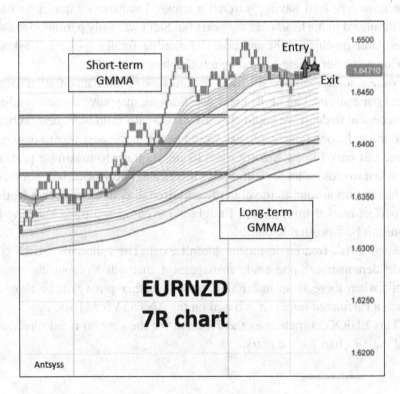

**Figure 16.1.**   EURNZD 7R chart.

**Figure 16.2.** EURNZD 3R chart.

practical solution is to manage the trade based on the information present on the chart at the time of entry.

Types of information include the following:

(1) **Trend Change** — A change in trend from your preferred indicator can be a warning sign to consider taking some profit or to close out your trade.

(2) **Obvious Support or Resistance Levels** — When price is unable to close above or below a certain price level, consider the possibility this level could be a turning point for price to go against your trade. If price manages to push past a previous level then there is the possibility for price to continue further in your direction.

This EURNZD long trade became profitable as price continued up. Price was not able to close above the 1.6495 resistance level. This was a sign of a potential price retreat so half the position was closed at 1.6495 to lock in a 15-pip profit. The Stop Loss moved to 1.6475 slightly below breakeven.

(3) **Emerging Price Patterns or Indicator Signals** — During a trade, the appearance of price patterns such as a Head and Shoulders alert you to the possibility of price travelling down in the future.

(4) **Stop Loss or Target Profit Attained** — These are the obvious price points calling a trader to action. Once price reaches the predetermined price, it is up to trader discipline to exit the trade. Or perhaps not exit the trade if there are other signs on the chart to leave the position open.

The remaining position on EURNZD was stopped out at 1.6475 when price moved down and triggered the recalculated Stop Loss. This resulted in a small loss of 5 pips.

If only I knew with 100% certainty price would not reach my 30-pip target. Knowing this piece of information, I would have closed the entire position at 1.6495 for a higher profit compared to closing half of the position and letting the remaining position run.

So my ultimate question for this particular trade is: when should I take my profit? The crystal ball answer is 15 pips.

We don't have a crystal ball to look forward, but it's very good at looking backwards. That's useful because it allows us to set a benchmark for trade returns and measure our performance against this. It can be demoralising. The objective is to use the rear-looking crystal ball to improve our trading going forward.

Escaping a bad trade should also be our greatest triumph.

*"What was your greatest espionage triumph against us?" General Cung's answer was not one of a great spy story but one of avoiding capture. When a dozen American helicopters landed unexpectedly near a house where Cung was meeting agents, there was no time to escape. The woman of the house led the men to an underground tunnel beneath the house. Despite interrogation and threats from the Americans to burn the woman with lit cigarettes, she simply said, "They slipped out through the bamboo when you landed."*

# Part 3

# Mind Matters

# Chapter 17

# "LOV" Gone Wrong

There is a natural tendency to get emotionally involved when a stock does well. We feel happiness when we think of it and just the thought of the stock makes us smile. In our mind, price only goes in one direction — up. It's blind love. However, as traders, we must pay attention to any warning signs we see on the chart and be prepared to take action.

Lovisa Holdings "LOV" had been a stock traders dream about. In less than a year, it doubled its value and it appeared to have no end to its potential for profit.

On the LOV Daily chart, Figure 17.1, we see the long-term GMMA lines are evenly separated on the chart with the long-term investors in strong support of the uptrend.

It's easy to fall in love with this trend action so a mid-trend entry is taken. At the entry point, the short-term GMMA lines have compressed. This shows where buyers and sellers reach a point of price agreement and where it is possible for the trend to change. Given the long-term GMMA shows strong support for the uptrend, it is highly probable for price to continue in the same direction.

The overall uptrend seen on the Weekly chart, Figure 17.2, is used to trade LOV. In order to find an entry point we go back to the Daily chart. The area of compression looks like a pullback in the overall uptrend and is a good area to enter the trade. A long trade on LOV is opened at an entry price of $5.23 with a 2*ATR weekly Stop Loss of $4.49 and a Profit Target of $6.01.

Price continued on upwards without closing below the weekly 2*ATR. Price reached a high of $12.53, more than double the original share price of $5.23. Before this high, half of the position was closed at $11.61 in

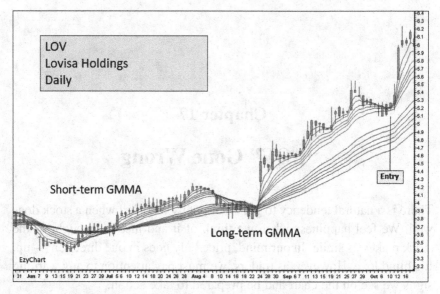

**Figure 17.1.** LOV Daily chart.

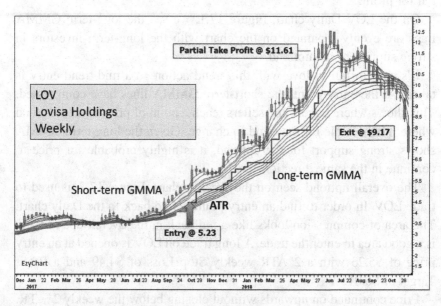

**Figure 17.2.** LOV Weekly chart.

order to lock in a return of 121%. The remaining position was left to run until the Stop Loss was hit.

A smooth, steady ride to the top was followed by a gradual decline where price fell through the weekly 2*ATR Stop Loss of $10.10 a number of times before actually closing below this price. By this stage, the warning signs were already in place, signalling a change. The short-term GMMA was turning downwards and beginning to pass through the long-term GMMA. A change in trend was taking place.

As price rose and fell around the 2*ATR Stop Loss price level of $10.10 for a few weeks, a false hope was created as I viewed this downturn as a temporary one only.

I fell in love with LOV as well as its potential for more profit, and this caused me to delay my exit. Instead of closing the trade on the next day after the stock price had closed under $10.10, I held on a little longer than necessary. The remaining open position on LOV was finally closed at $9.17 for a return of 75%.

This trade was influenced by feelings of love, leading to hesitation in closing the trade when the Stop Loss price was hit. When developing a trading plan, we are usually in a logical frame of mind. The trading plan is our guide to decision-making without emotion. We should obey our trading plan. My love for LOV profits kept me in the trade. Following the chart and not our heart most often results in consistent profits.

Making money shouldn't be our main focus in a trade. We need to switch off from these thoughts of money and focus more on what the chart is telling us.

# Chapter 18

# Don't Show Me the Money

In the movie *Jerry Maguire*, Cuba Gooding Jr and Tom Cruise play characters whose dialogue develops into a crescendo of emotion as they shout, "Show me the money!" The markets often call to us in the same way. It's a euphoric feeling when we are in profit but a stomach churning one when it's not. I found it better to switch off from the crazed emotional "show me the money" in order to focus on the chart and rational management of the trade.

In the days before live trading screens, brokers had a ticker machine that delivered current prices. Many traders refused to have these machines because as they said, "Eventually you will feed it money." Avoiding this reflex action is even more of a challenge today when on-screen tickers show your profit or loss tick by tick.

The ANTSSYS 321 trade on a GBDAUD trade shows how this strategy is applied. I used an 8R chart for the general direction, a 5R chart for the medium-term confirmation, and a 3R chart for my entry.

On the right side of the 8R chart, Figure 18.1, the short-term GMMA had earlier compressed, turned, and passed down through the long-term GMMA. A downward trend change had occurred with the long-term GMMA now sitting above the short-term GMMA.

Based on a 3R chart, a short trade was entered into at 1.9889 with a Stop Loss at 1.9909 and a Take Profit target at 1.9859.

ANTSSYS uses range bar charts which reduce price action noise with fewer bars plotting only significant price movement.

In order to reduce further trading noise and the distraction of "show me the money", I hid the Trading Panel on my trading platform. The panel provides real-time details of my open profits and open losses.

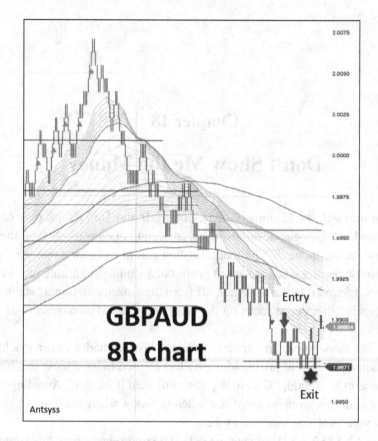

**Figure 18.1.** GBPAUD 8R chart.

Previously I would have had my eye on the "money", my open profit or losses. Minute by minute I would be riding the emotional rollercoaster associated with watching diminishing or increasing profits or losses.

However, with the trading panel closed, I could only look to the chart to tell me what was happening. Decisions were not based on fear or greed or how many dollars I was losing or gaining, just purely based on indicators and price action.

The 8R chart had kept me in the trade until I realised my 30-pip target price was not going to be met. When price was unable to sustain the breakthrough for a third time, I quickly closed the trade, locking in a profit. The star on the 8R chart, Figure 18.1, marks the exit.

Show me the money? Showing price action and indicators minus the open profit or loss directs your focus to what is happening on the chart while removing distracting emotions from the trade.

It isn't only about money and it isn't about getting everything right in every trade either. Managing our trades and making the best decisions at the time can also be considered a mark of success in trading.

Watching the money monitor instead of the price chart is one obstacle on the path to success. Another is the trade post-mortem when the focus is on trade perfection.

Natural curiosity drives us to contemplate price long after a trade has been closed. We look at the potential for more yield after an exit, what the best exit price was, and whether the current price action has reinforced our original decision. There is nothing more satisfying than watching price collapse just after you exit a trade. However, the measure of success in a trade isn't always about exit and profit perfection.

We use an example trade as a base for comparison to examine different scenarios where the post-mortem is about trade improvement rather than perfection.

My entry for this trade is based on the Daily chart, Figure 18.2. The short-term GMMA expanded after a short period of compression just before the marked entry. A new leg in the uptrend was emerging. I opened a trade on MDL at 0.73 with a Stop Loss of 0.67 based on a 1*ATR on the Daily chart and a Target Profit of 0.85.

Price continued to trend upwards towards 0.865, presenting an opportunity to close the trade for a profit of 18.4%. The target profit had already been achieved but I decided to let profits run and to close the trade only if price closed on or below the 1*ATR Stop Loss on the Daily chart.

When your trade is already in the money, the original capital outlay is no longer at risk. Using the 1*ATR line as a trailing profit, Stop Loss enables the profits to run further. It's a suitable strategy because only the profit is at risk.

After hitting 0.865, price started to move sideways and the 1*ATR Stop Loss was triggered intraday at 0.78. The following day, I closed the trade on MDL at 0.81. In hindsight, a trading error had occurred. I had not waited for price to close below the 1*ATR line as planned and price continued moving up to a new high of 0.89.

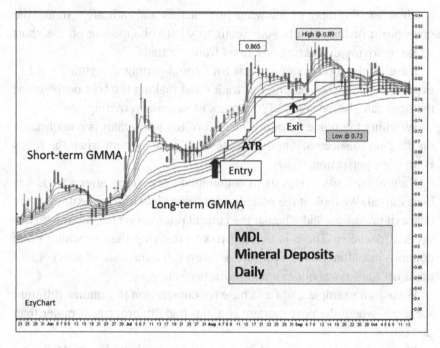

**Figure 18.2.** MDL Daily chart.

It's true the road to perfection is always under construction. My road to perfection already had a pothole. Further construction in terms of paying more attention to detail on the chart and discipline in trade management was required for future trades.

Table 18.1 shows the results of different scenarios if the trade remained open.

Capturing the highest price at 0.89 yields a return of 21.92%. This is the Maximum Potential Profit.

A falling sell order triggered on the intraday low of 0.73 yields a break-even return. The Maximum Potential Loss is not a capital loss but it's not exactly a good situation to find yourself back to square one.

In retrospect, I was satisfied with the outcome despite the pothole.

In summary:

(1) My short-term trade returned a 10.96% profit.
(2) I avoided going back to 0% return.

**Table 18.1.** Exit outcomes.

| Trade Scenarios | Entry Price | Exit Price | Profit/Loss |
|---|---|---|---|
| 1*ATR Daily End of Day Stop Loss Triggered | 0.73 | 0.81 | 0.08 |
| Maximum Potential Profit | 0.73 | 0.89 | 0.16 |
| Maximum Potential Loss | 0.73 | 0.73 | 0 |

(3) A 21.92% profit opportunity presented itself after my trade was closed.

I managed to achieve points (1) and (2). I made a profit without going back to zero and as Meatloaf famously sings, "Now don't be sad, cause two out of three ain't bad."

We aim for perfection in our trading and sometimes fall short. Perfection under circumstances beyond our control is not always possible. Better trade plans and chart analysis are solutions we continually work on. In this MDL trade, achieving two out of three and not perfection still gives very good results.

Effective execution of the trading plan is the focus and not the need to be perfectly right. Perfection is defined as being correct in every way. It also means the process of improving to make something perfect. We probably won't get to the ultimate state of trade perfection but striving to improve our trading results is part of the process of perfection.

The trader's focus is on the chart. We should always listen to our chart.

# Chapter 19

# Listen to Your Chart

A chart, like a picture, is worth a thousand words. It reveals the "story" of a stock. Every impact from any event or fundamental data release leaves price footprints on the chart. The price chart shows us what price is doing without the need to know the reasons why. Technical analysis of the chart helps us understand how price may behave in the future.

It's called listening to the chart, but what does this mean in practice? The following trade on Afterpay Touch (APT) illustrates how to listen to the chart. It's also a cautionary story of what happens when chart signals are discounted because of a news announcement. Listening to distractions means a trade is backed by an element of emotional attachment encouraged by investment gurus but fatal for traders. As a technical trader, letting emotion or news influence a trade is not a good idea. This is a trap to avoid and APT captures these errors.

The APT Daily chart, Figure 19.1, shows a pullback in price together with a compression of the short-term GMMA. Traders were coming to an agreement in price. A breakout in price usually occurs after a compression. For this trade, the breakout in price was more likely to be to the upside considering the uptrend of the short-term GMMA on the Weekly chart, Figure 19.2. APT did not have a long-term GMMA yet on the Weekly chart as it was a newly traded stock and there was insufficient data to plot the long-term GMMA lines. A trade on APT was opened at the price of $5.46 and a Target Profit of $6.31 set using the Weekly chart.

A trailing 1*ATR Stop Loss on the Weekly chart is used to manage the trade. A close below the ATR is an exit signal with an exit taken on the next day. When price closed exactly on $4.80, it was a borderline situation requiring assessment on the following day when markets opened.

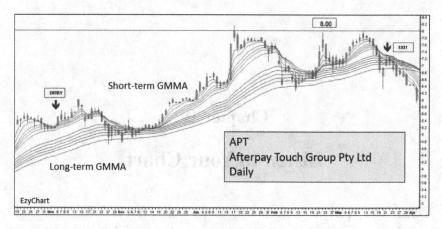

**Figure 19.1.**  APT Daily chart.

Price bounced off this Stop Loss level of $4.80 so the position was kept open as it was a good sign of buyer activity in the market. The ATR Stop Loss was recalculated.

Prices continued to climb and Stop Loss number 2 at $6.89 was triggered. This should have been the day to close the trade but fundamental information got in the way. It was 10 days before the Half Year Reports were due. Leaving the trade open, I imagined reaping the rewards of a good report.

This was mistake number one. Taking into account other information outside the chart when this trade was one based on technical analysis management is not part of the trading plan. Regardless, I wanted to wait until APT reported.

Mistake number two was when the emotional attachment set in. Afterpay provided a platform service using the concept of a "shop now, take now, pay it in 4" instalments basis to which many thousands of retailers were associated. The Afterpay logo was prolific online as well as in-store. Some of the biggest retailers were using the Afterpay service. Shopping can be an emotional experience and seeing all my favourite stores using this service cemented my emotional attachment to this company. It's the Warren Buffet approach — buy companies you know from experience. Surely APT would report good earnings, I reasoned so the ATR Stop Loss was recalculated once again.

The two days leading into the day of the earnings report saw APT's price rise to a high of $8.00, giving a total rise of 13.2%.

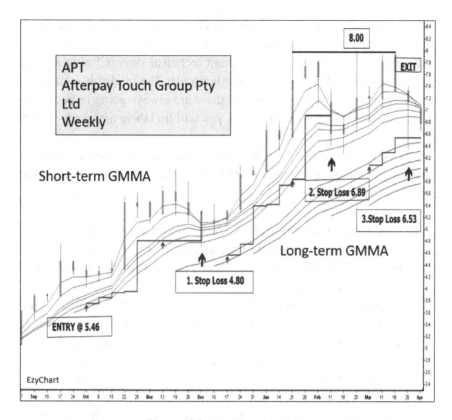

**Figure 19.2.** APT Weekly chart.

A few weeks later, the third ATR Stop Loss on the Weekly chart was hit at $6.53. Despite APT having presented a highly favourable earnings report, the charts were telling me a different story. The days leading up to the third ATR Stop Loss saw APT's share price drop around 12%.

Analysing the Weekly and the Daily charts on a post-trade basis, price had made three attempts to break through the resistance level at $8.00. On the Daily chart, the short-term GMMAs were beginning to turn over and downwards into the long-term GMMAs. The warning signs were written all over the chart but I wasn't listening. Given this was the third time of hitting the ATR Stop Loss, I had run out of excuses and could no longer hold onto the notion that this was still a great stock. I closed the trade at $6.53 for a 19% profit.

If I had solely listened to my chart, the APT trade would have been closed on Stop Loss point number 2 at $6.89 giving a higher return of 26% profit.

APT was still the same company with the great concepts that had provided additional reasons for me to hold the stock. However, if you listen
to the chart, it is telling a very different technical story. Closing a trade
enables us to go fishing again for another trade. The market is a huge sea
of opportunity for finding trades and there are always going to be fish to
catch. Every time you look for trades, you will find there are plenty of fish
in the sea.

In the last few chapters, we have discussed how mind matters play an
important role in our endeavour to trade successfully. The main factors for
consideration are as follows:

(1) **Missed trades don't matter** — There is never a rush to place a trade.
    Remember trade opportunities are as common as the number of fish
    in the sea. The trade you missed today will not be the last profitable
    one you will ever see.

(2) **Perfect profits are impossible** — A perfect life is impossible as is the
    perfect profit. Yes there might have been more profit if you held on
    and maybe you could have captured the highest price but if you didn't
    it isn't an indication of a faulty trade. If you managed to make a profit
    then you probably made the right decisions at the time in order to
    capture it. Hindsight is perfect. Real life trading isn't.

(3) **Setting stops is essential** — A Stop Loss based on technical factors
    removes the emotion from the decision of when a trade should be
    closed. We can't fall in love with our stocks. Holding on can cause us
    to fall into loss or further into larger losses. More time spent on ana-
    lysing the charts, and not on how much money we are making, leads
    to more rational decision-making.

(4) **Trade discipline makes you a winner** — Setting and following the
    rules you set up for yourself will make you a more organised and
    focused trader. A trader who sets up a good trading plan knows when
    to let profits run and, more importantly, knows when to close a trade
    to limit losses when they are wrong.

Be aware of these mind matters in your trading. These are not for the
goal of trade perfection but for better trading, small losses, and satisfying
profits.

# Part 4

# Stepping Up to FX

# Chapter 20

# Greener Pastures

The time for adding foreign currency (FX) to trading strategies has arrived. The reason is the enduring changed structure of the markets following the global financial crisis (GFC). What worked before the GFC is no longer as effective.

The GFC was the equivalent of the 1929 market crash. That crash give birth to new ways of understanding markets, starting with John Maynard Keynes and *The General Theory of Employment, Interest and Money*. It changed our understanding of markets and investors like Warren Buffet have benefited from these insights.

The 2008 GFC has not given birth to any new ways of understanding markets. It has given birth to new trading instruments including an explosion of Exchange Traded Funds (ETFs) and High Frequency Trading (HFT). Advances in technology have made derivative markets accessible for ordinary traders using contract for differences (CFDs) and FX.

However, financial advisors remain wedded to methodologies based on the Benjamin Graham and David Dodd classic *Security Analysis*, published in the same year as the pilots' flight manual for the new Spitfire fighter. The principles of flight remain unchanged, but no modern pilot would use the 1936 Spitfire manual to fly an F18 fighter. Yet investment advisors continue to rely on Dodd and Graham methodologies despite changed market conditions.

Markets and market opportunities have changed so it's time for traders to add some greener pastures in their trading repertoire. To understand why we need to move to greener pastures, we start by looking at what has poisoned the previous pastures.

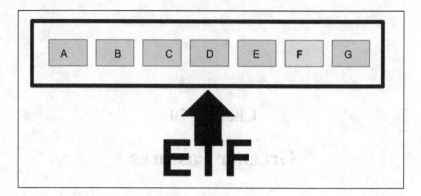

**Figure 20.1.**   Exchange traded funds.

## Exchange Traded Funds

By some estimates, ETF trading accounts for around 40% of all trading activity in the market. The growth of ETFs sucks liquidity out of the market because ownership is concentrated in ETFs. There are fewer mid-cap stocks not included in an ETF. There are even fewer traders involved in the more speculative end of the market. There are fewer and fewer stocks and people to trade with outside of ETF holdings.

An ETF holds a basket of stocks. Instructions from ETF holders force the ETF to buy or sell the entire basket of stocks so the ratio of stocks held remains constant. Irrespective of an individual stocks' performance, good or bad, all the stocks in the ETF basket are bought or sold to maintain the portfolio ratio.

Traders holding stock F in Figure 20.1 may find it sold down in response to ETF activity despite having a well-established uptrend. This kills individual trades and makes equity trading more difficult.

There are alternative methods of trading ETFs and these are more fully examined in **Guppy Trading**.

This ETF activity effects volatility behaviour and trend stability. This behaviour is exacerbated by the HFT traders.

## High Frequency Trading

HFT appears to be legalised front running. HFT, by some estimates, now accounts for nearly 60% of trading volume on the New York Stock

Exchange (NYSE). Start with 40% for ETF and nearly 60% for HFT trading, there is just a sliver of trading activity attributable to retail investors.

Figure 20.2 shows how HFT front running works.

We start with old fashioned front running shown by the lower line between the broker and the market. You place your order with the broker. The broker knew you were a good trader, so he simply put his order in front of your order and got a better fill. You got a slightly worse price. It was often called slippage but is still illegal.

Enter HFT traders. They get between the brokers' transmission of your order and its placement in the order line as it goes to market. The delay in transmission — latency — expands the further away the broker is from the exchange. The HFT trader makes a split-second intervention, tapping into the transmission of the order from the broker to the exchange order book. They place their order in front of the intercepted order. It is high speed front running. They buy a fraction of a second before your order and at a slightly better price. Then they sell back to you at a small a profit. Do this thousands of times and the scalps add up to make a very profitable business.

This legalised hacking is facilitated by the Exchanges selling fast access tools to the highest bidder. The HFT traders pay to sit next to, or inside, the exchange data rooms to reduce latency and get an edge over their competitors.

Liquidity volume is where HFT and ETF come together. They are not scalping your order for 1,200 shares. They are scalping the ETF initiated order causing a large volume adjustment across a portfolio of shares. The combination of ETF orders makes HFT possible. The HFT traders feed off large volume orders from ETF and institutional fund managers.

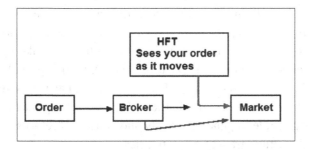

**Figure 20.2.** High frequency trading.

This combination changes the nature of volatility in the market. In 1970, the average holding period for stocks on the NYSE was four years. In 2008, the average holding period was two months. In 2011, with the growth of HFT, the average holding period was 22 seconds! The impact of HFT trading cannot be ignored. The underlying trend may look relatively stable, but on an intraday basis, the price activity is clustered around ETF and HFT activity.

The bulk of the price move takes place in the first or last five to 10 minutes of trading. In between these periods the price drifts sideways. One strategy is to enter near the end of the day and ride the volatility gap the next day using a CFD. Great if price moves up rapidly and you are long. Not so good price if moves up rapidly and you are short. Taking overnight CFD positions now has an increased level of risk.

## GFC PTSD Hangover

The GFC was a long time ago, but enhanced by the growth of ETF and HFT activity, the Post Traumatic Stress Disorder continues. This combination of factors changes the profile of the market. Pre-GFC the market sloped more or less evenly from the deep liquid end to the shallow end. There was a good pool of trading opportunities in the middle of this slope. After the GFC, the profile has a very deep end and a very shallow end. There is no gradual slope as shown in Figure 20.3. The shallow end offers very few trading opportunities. The deep end liquidity is populated by ETFs and HFT traders. It's difficult to compete with these traders or to find useful trading opportunities that are not suddenly destroyed by the impacts of these large traders.

Ultimately the nature and range of opportunities in the equity market have diminished. It has become more difficult to generate consistent returns from trading equity markets. Even if we transfer equity analysis and execution to a CFD market, the volatility changes make it more difficult to enter and generate good returns. The FX market provides a viable alternative because it is deep, liquid, and it does not have the same volatility characteristics as the equity markets. The trading approaches are scalable so it is possible to generate steady and consistent returns without the need to find multiple trading opportunities.

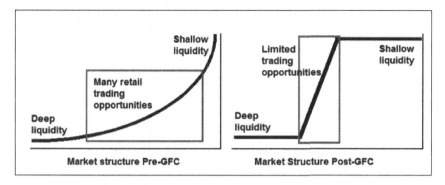

**Figure 20.3.** Changing market structure.

FX markets have specific characteristics very different from equity markets. The idea that you make your fortune trading equities and then lose it learning to trade FX is a path we want to avoid. Our understanding of the way the FX market works, and the appropriate trading solutions, are not the standard solutions found in most FX books. These greener pastures may be toxic, so caution is needed. In Chapter 21, we take you through the important differences and the lessons required for developing a sustainable FX trading strategy to augment returns from equity trading.

# Chapter 21

# Stepping Up to FX

The step-up from trading ordinary stocks to trading leveraged derivatives is not a small leap. The same base skills are required, including good trade and trend identification. However, the discipline of even the best equity traders is tested in a derivative trading environment, be it CFDs or FX or futures. These markets soon tell you if your trade discipline is good enough, or if you have just been fooling yourself with luck. The leverage in these trading instruments magnifies your every weakness, making these markets unsuitable for beginner traders.

Moving from equities to derivatives turns you into, if not a beginner, at least a pre-schooler again. There are four essential considerations when equity traders step-up to FX and derivatives trading.

The first consideration is the idea the FX market is not dissimilar to the equity market — it just moves more quickly so therefore traders need to act more quickly. It's true, there are periods when the FX market moves very quickly on an intraday basis. News is instantly incorporated into the price activity in a 24-hour market. A major announcement such as Chinese PMI figures is channelled into quite a small number of currency trading pairs. The result is a rapid move and adjustment.

In the equity market, the same news impacts flow unevenly. It may affect iron ore miners and exporters but has limited impact on banks. Although individual stocks may move quickly, there is usually a limited impact on the broader market as most stocks are not affected by Chinese PMI.

The FX market is not constantly reacting to news and reports. There are extended periods of mind-numbing boredom as currency pairs barely move.

The appearance of the need for speed is created, in part, by the higher levels of leverage available in FX trading. Losses grow very quickly if stops are not acted on rapidly and with absolute discipline. Profits disappear quickly if Take-Profit stops are not applied. The magnification of price consequences through leverage helps to create the impression of speed.

Trading the FX market does not mean applying equity trading techniques at a faster rate. Many equity trading techniques do not succeed in the FX market no matter how fast you try to apply them. Speed is not the foundation of success in the FX market.

The second consideration is the nature of the FX markets. When you walk into a bank and exchange $10,000 Australian dollars for the equivalent in US dollars, you force the bank into an FX transaction. They are forced to buy US dollars at a time when they may much prefer to sell US dollars against the Australian dollar, but your order gives them no choice. They must take the other side of the trade even if they think it is the wrong side of the market to be on. Your $10,000 is a small amount, but multiply these transactions with other individuals and with companies and you get a better picture. Around half of the participants in the FX market are taking the other side of a currency trade because they have to, not because they believe this is a smart trade.

Banks and others hedge their currency risk using a variety of methods, but this is also a direct result of their involuntary activity in the FX market created by business demands for currency exchange services.

Compare this with the stock market. If you decide to buy a bank stock then you buy it from a willing seller. The seller sells because they believe the trend will move in the opposite direction or they believe the profit they have is already ample. They are not forced to sell.

This market of willing participants has a very important implication, making the equity market a psychological playground. Price is a psychological artefact produced by our fears and hopes. Our equity trading techniques focus on understanding the psychological behaviour of buyers and sellers revealed in a range of chart patterns capturing the changing dynamic of supply and demand. Many technical indicators also have a sound psychological basis. These are discussed in my book *Chart Trading*.

These are profound differences between the FX and the equity market, so the psychological trade analysis applied to equity markets is less successful in FX markets. In equity markets, traders are not forced to take a long or short position so patterns of price behaviour accurately reflect the psychology of traders. Chart patterns reflect the psychology of market participants (Figure 21.1). In FX markets, chart patterns are discounted because the number of unwilling participants distorts the psychological behaviour. This discounting is shown in several of the FX trades in previous chapters. The trades have been constructed around the head and shoulder pattern, but the entry conditions confirmed with other indicators.

Pattern 1 is a head and shoulder pattern. It reflects the decline of enthusiasm in the market, showing a loss of momentum and confidence. This is used as a reliable pattern in equity markets because it captures the psychological behaviour of participants. When used in the FX market, this pattern acts as a guide.

Pattern 2 is a rounding top. It reflects the gradual decline of confidence in the market. Equity investors lose enthusiasm and gradually become

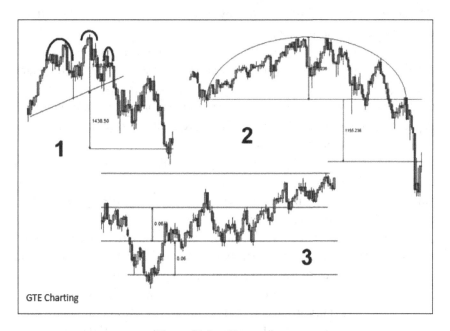

**Figure 21.1.** Chart patterns.

sellers. The pattern captures the behaviour of market participants as they assess the changes in market conditions. This pattern also appears in FX markets but again has no strong nor reliably implied meaning.

Many traders feel frustrated because they have observed head and shoulder patterns, rounding top, up sloping triangles, and other patterns in the FX markets. These are coincidental patterns of price behaviour and they do not contain the psychological behavioural input these patterns have in the equity market. The result? A head and shoulder pattern in an FX market does not lead to a market collapse with projected downside targets.

This is a core difference between FX and equity markets. It is a direct result of the make-up of the FX market with its high level of unwilling participants. Our FX trading and analysis methods are constructed around different market features where support and resistance and trend lines become the dominant analysis features.

Pattern 3 often appears in FX markets. It is a simple pattern of support and resistance. In equity markets, this psychological pattern reflects the way participants make decisions around their entry price. It becomes a reference anchor against which they measure profits and losses. It's a direct psychological pattern.

However, we cannot assign the same psychological foundations to the pattern. FX participants do not reference a buy or sell point in the Euro Dollar in the same way they do with an equity as there are few very long-term positions. We do not have a good explanation for the dominance of support and resistance lines in the FX market, but this does not prevent us from making use of these features.

The FX market is effectively analysed using support and resistance levels — trading bands — and trend analysis. These tools may appear too simple to apply to a complex FX market, but in reality, they give effective and reliable analysis and trading solutions.

The third consideration relates to inside or informed trading. Regrettably, this is an entrenched feature of equity markets and traders develop specific strategies and tactics to recognise when it's happening so they can decide if they want to participate in the move or avoid the stock completely.

There is essentially no inside trading in the FX market, although conspiracy theories may abound (Figure 21.2). The two AUD-pair charts

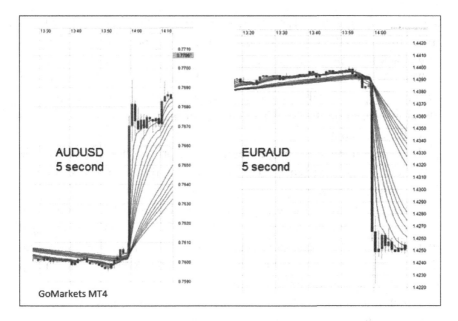

**Figure 21.2.**   No inside trading.

show exactly the same behaviour in response to a single news event. Inside trading was alleged by the market regulators, but this was wrong as all AUD currency pairs reacted in the same way at the same time. This clearly showed the relevant news story was released to the market a few seconds before the official release time.      •

There is no doubt the FX market is manipulated by the banks. Court judgements against many of the banking giants, such as HSBC, Deutsche Bank, and others, have revealed a widespread culture of market manipulation.

However, this doesn't impact retail FX traders because our planned exposure to the market is measured in hours, not days or weeks. We are not involved in hedging, so market manipulation is just a background feature of the ocean in which we are surfing.

Markets at all levels are manipulated by the overt or covert behaviour of banks and funds. We need to work within this environment and, at the same time, encourage regulators to accept the facts rather than denying them.

The fourth consideration is the 24-hour FX market with multiple opens. Risk management is more difficult as markets trade when we want to sleep, so we adjust the types of trading opportunities we use. This has a major impact on the way we choose to trade. To understand why, we need to go back to some basics.

The FX market is a 24-hour market with multiple opens. The choice of the opening price for the candle display on a Daily chart is very arbitrary. Usually it based on the New York open, but there is no sound reason for this. It's just a convenience.

The chart on the left shows the actual daily price activity in each of the New York, Asian, and European markets during their one day of trading. Each candle is different.

What is more disconcerting is when we look at the 24-hour composite daily candle. If the starting point for the full 24-hour candle is changed then the shape of the candle is very different. Its bearish if we start with the New York open. Its bullish if we start with the Asia open, and a doji candle if we start with the UK open.

Which one is correct? The meaning of each candle is very different. This suggests we need to apply classic equity-derived candle chart analysis with caution. When it comes to applying candle pattern analysis to FX charts, then its simply a nonsense because the daily pattern changes depending on your selected starting time (Figure 21.3).

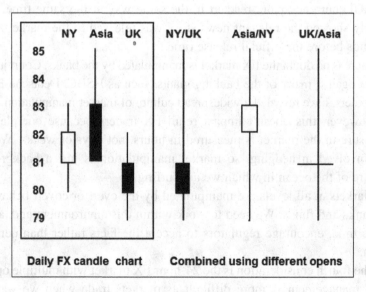

**Figure 21.3.**  Calculating FX candles.

One solution uses a chart based on price activity and not on the arbitrarily selected "open" for the market. These are point and figure and range bar solutions discussed in later chapters.

The very problem of a 24-hour market and how to select the correct candle start time paves the way for a trading solution taking us to the very core of the way we prefer to trade FX markets. Our preference is for short-term tactical trading giving 50–160 pips for each trade.

This means we need to get the entry and the exit consistently correct. This is a more demanding task than when we trade equities where any slippage is not magnified by instrument leverage. We use position size — not the number of trades — to generate the profit. These short-term trades use a 3- or 10- or 30-minute candle chart so there is no dispute over the correct open and close price levels for each candle.

Starting in Chapter 23, we explain the methods used to deliver good returns from short-term trades usually lasting one to three hours.

## Chapter 22

# High Probability FX

Moving from trading equities to trading FX calls for old skills applied in new ways. The objective is to develop a high probability selection method with defined targets for trades lasting three to five hours. There are four elements required to develop this method.

1. First is a selection process to identify high probability trades and targets.
2. Second is an appropriate analysis method.
3. Third is a Stop Loss method to protect capital and open profits as the trade moves towards the target level.
4. The fourth is any refinement to enhance accuracy.

With suitable modification, we bring established trading skills to this task. In equity markets, we are faced with thousands of stocks so we must develop methods to drill down and isolate the best opportunities. For the FX market, we apply a simple statistical concept to quickly identify the top five trading candidates and shift rapidly to analysis and trade execution.

The 5-day Average Daily Range (5 ADR) is the Swiss army knife in the ANTS-Lite FX trading approach. It not only provides a method to isolate the best opportunities, but also delivers a profitable and enduring statistical relationship.

There is an 85% probability the next day's price move will reach 75% of the 5-day ADR value. You probably need to pause and read the previous sentence again because this shifts the odds of success massively in your favour. We use this for Index, commodity, and FX trading.

The 5-day ADR delivers a statistical relationship with an 85% probability of achieving 75% of the value of the 5-day ADR in the next 24–48 hours. The higher the value, the greater the potential price move and profit. ADR calculations are used to identify and rank potential trading candidates. Every day the ADR values are posted on www. guppytraders.com.

Figure 22.1 shows how the ADR is calculated.

The ADR calculation should not be confused with the Average True Range (ATR) calculation developed by Welles Wilder. The ADR calculation is a simple moving average of the price range over the past five days.

The most important measure in the FX market is the price range. This is the daily value of the difference between the high and the low of each day. Time in the FX market is a major risk factor so we need to find strong and quick price moves. The first step establishes the recent ranging activity of each pair. This reduces the number of pairs we need to look at in the same way a stock search is used to create a smaller pool of stocks suitable for trading.

The trade opportunity identification starts by ranking the currency pairs according to their 5-day average range. Pairs with a 5-ADR below 100 are ignored. Our focus is on the major pairs rather than little known currencies. We aim to capture 75% of the GBPAUD 5-ADR value of 149 pips in Figure 22.2 because it offers the potential for a 112-pip trade.

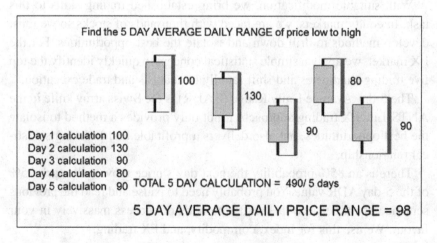

Figure 22.1. ADR calculation.

| | Pips |
|---|---|
| GBPAUD | 149 |
| GBPCAD | 145 |
| GBPNZD | 144 |
| EURCAD | 123 |
| EURAUD | 119 |
| EURNZD | 115 |
| AUDCAD | 98 |
| GBPCHF | 82 |
| NZDCAD | 78 |

**Figure 22.2.** Pip values.

Of course, there is a problem. This statistical relationship gives the potential range of price activity, but it does not point to the direction of the move. Further analysis is required to identify the best directional trade and it's not always the pair with the highest ADR. This analysis rests on our previously developed equity trading skills and we look at how these are adapted in the next chapter, but first a diversion is necessary.

## A Diversion

There is a question captured in the gleam of your eye and it needs an answer. Can this be applied to equity trading?

The answer is "Yes", but remember this is designed to capture a one-day trade. This is not rally or trend trading. The ADR ranges are typically smaller, so this disadvantage is overcome by executing the trade using a derivative such as a CFD for leverage. Restricting the ADR rankings reach to only those stocks covered by a CFD reduces the size of the analysis pool.

We start with a basic Metastock exploration. Coding is shown below. The objective is to first find the value of the 5-day average range of price. We use AAAA as the base example.

The high low range for five days is shown in Figure 22.3. The total range is 304 and the 5-day average range value is 60.8. The 75% value of this is $0.46. This means there is an 85% probability of tomorrow's price reaching 75% of the 5-day average range with a move of $0.46.

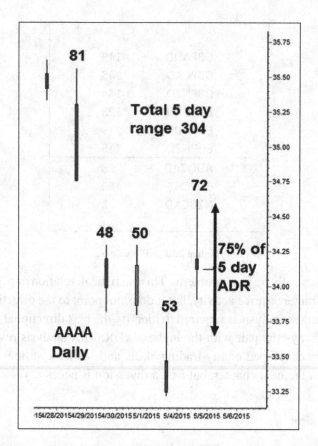

**Figure 22.3.**   5-day ADR.

The AAAA chart highlights the issue of price gaps with the application of 5-day ADR to equity markets. The 5-day ADR calculation ignores price gaps. If the AAAA price gaps go down today and opens at $33.50, then the price range remains at $0.46 above or below the open price.

This is a small 1.35% move. It's not worth trading as a direct equity trade. However, with 10% leverage from a CFD, this result is boosted to 13.5%. This takes us to the next step in using the Metastock equities exploration.

It's not useful to rank exploration results based on the raw 5-day ADR. Whilst a move of $0.46 is not particularly useful in a $34 stock, it's much more significant in a $10 stock as these stocks often have 25% CFD leverage.

The exploration is modified to express the gain of $0.46 as a percentage rise based on the current close price. Again, the figures are generally small, but they are boosted by derivative leverage.

We further refine the list by grouping stocks into cohorts. The first list in Figure 22.4 shows stocks trading between $5.00 and $15.00. These mid-cap stocks usually attract 25% CFD leverage.

The second list in Figure 22.5 includes stock trading between $15.00 and $40.00. These blue chips usually come with CFD leverage of 10%.

**"5 day average range %" Explored**

Results | Rejects | Exploration

| Security Name | ADR% | cents | close | Ticker |
|---|---|---|---|---|
| ASTROJAPAN-STAPL | 3.8425 | 0.2025 | 5.2700 | AJA |
| PXUTRUST PREF | 3.4500 | 0.3105 | 9.0000 | PXUPA |
| MINERAL RSRCS | 3.3991 | 0.2325 | 6.8400 | MIN |
| TPG TELECOM-FPO | 2.9352 | 0.2580 | 8.7900 | TPM |
| SILVER CHEF LMTD | 2.8696 | 0.2640 | 9.2000 | SIV |
| MONADELPHOUS GRP | 2.8354 | 0.2790 | 9.8400 | MND |
| NUFARM LIMITED | 2.7866 | 0.2115 | 7.5900 | NUF |
| SEVEN GRP-FPO | 2.6815 | 0.1995 | 7.4400 | SVW |

Metastock

**Figure 22.4.** Midcap ADR rankings.

**"5 day average range %" Explored**

Results | Rejects | Exploration

| Security Name | ADR% | cents | close | Ticker |
|---|---|---|---|---|
| SIRTEX MEDICAL | 3.1753 | 0.6465 | 20.3600 | SRX |
| ANSELL LIMITED | 2.6336 | 0.6900 | 26.2000 | ANN |
| MGLLN FN GRP LTD | 2.2289 | 0.4440 | 19.9200 | MFG |
| LEND LEASE-STAPLED | 2.2246 | 0.3675 | 16.5200 | LLC |
| JB HI FI LIMITED | 2.1050 | 0.4050 | 19.2400 | JBH |
| ISHR SPASX HIGH DIV | 1.9931 | 0.3195 | 16.0300 | IHD |
| ORICA LIMITED | 1.8354 | 0.3735 | 20.3500 | ORI |
| SONIC HEALTHCARE | 1.7976 | 0.3570 | 19.8600 | SHL |

Metastock

**Figure 22.5.** Blue chip ADR rankings.

**Table 22.1.** ADR performance.

| Midcap | Code | Today Open | ADR 75% | Target | Result |
|---|---|---|---|---|---|
| | | **ADR Equity Performance Tracking** | | | |
| | AJA | 5.29 | 0.2025 | 5.09 | 0 |
| | MIN | 6.82 | 0.2325 | 7.05 | 0 |
| | TPM | 8.59 | 0.2580 | 8.85 | 1 |
| | SIV | 9.19 | 0.2640 | 9.45 | 0 |
| | MND | 9.83 | 0.2790 | 10.11 | 0 |
| | | | | | |
| Bluechip | Code | Today Open | ADR 75% | Target | Result |
| | SRX | 20.00 | 0.6465 | 19.35 | 1 |
| | ANN | 25.92 | 0.6900 | 26.61 | 1 |
| | MFG | 19.20 | 0.4440 | 18.76 | 1 |
| | LLC | 2.56 | 0.3675 | 2.19 | 0 |
| | JBH | 19.10 | 0.4050 | 18.70 | 1 |
| | | | | | |
| Blue chip reach target range % | | | 90% | | |
| Midcap reach target range % | | | 10% | | |

The top 5–10 ADR figures are the starting point for closer chart examination. These are the stocks we are interested in trading and we apply the usual technical analysis to refine the opportunity, but we execute the trade using a CFD to go long or short. These are designed as short-term 1–3 days trades.

Table 22.1 shows the price moves on the day following this search. Those reaching target are marked 1. The method is less effective with mid-cap stocks but has very good results with blue chip stocks. This is a function of liquidity and the concentration of trading activity as a result of ETF trading.

The best directional trade is not always found with the highest ADR. This trend analysis starts with equity trading skills and we look at how these are adapted in Chapter 23.

**METASTOCK CODING**

Exploration code 5 Day Average Range ranked by %

**Col A: ADR%**

((((((HIGH-LOW)+((Ref(HIGH,-1))–(Ref(LOW, −1))) +((Ref(HIGH, −2))
−(Ref(LOW, −2))) +((Ref(HIGH, −3)) −(Ref(LOW,-3))) +((Ref(HIGH, −4))
(Ref(LOW,4))))/5)*75)/100)/CLOSE)*100

**Col B: cents**

((((HIGH-LOW) +((Ref(HIGH, −1))-(Ref(LOW, −1))) +((Ref(HIGH, −2))
−(Ref(LOW, −2))) +((Ref(HIGH, −3)) −(Ref(LOW, −3))) +((Ref(HIGH, −4))
−(Ref(LOW, −4))))/5)*75)/100

**Col C: close**

CLOSE

**Filter**

(colA/CLOSE)*100

# Chapter 23

# Guppy FX

With just five FX pairs candidates, the analysis process is rapid. The ADR selection method selects candidates with the potential to move substantially during the trading session, but the direction is unconfirmed. We draw on equity trend analysis skills to provide the trend direction solution before applying a Stop Loss method to protect capital and open profits as the trade moves towards the target level.

Previous chapters have included trades using the GMMA indicator, so we avoid unnecessary detail here. The purpose is to show how this trend analysis indicator is used to identify the direction of price movement in the five selected currency pairs.

The GMMA is made up of two groups of averages and, for convenience, we label them as traders and investors. The short-term group provides an indication of the way short-term traders are thinking. They are constructed from a group of 3, 5, 8, 10, 12, and 15 period exponential moving averages. The long-term group indicates the way investors are thinking. They use a cluster of 30, 35, 40, 45, 50, and 60 period exponential moving averages.

Agreement about price and value is shown when both groups of averages compress. The development of the compression creates an entry window, illustrated in Figure 23.1. The entry window is very near to the pivot point low of the trend. This is the absolute trend low, and is only identified retrospectively.

Aggressive traders enter in anticipation of the trend change. Conservative traders wait until the trend change is confirmed.

The degree and nature of expansion in each group of averages, and the gap between the groups of averages, help identify trend strength and stability. A full discussion of the GMMA is in *Guppy Trading*.

149

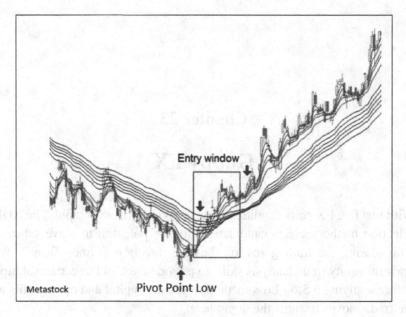

**Figure 23.1.** Guppy multiple moving average.

Usually the GMMA is applied to a Daily chart where each candle represents one day, and this is the method we apply for initial strategic analysis of the FX pairs. No surprises here so equity trading skills are applied without modification.

One of the essential differences between equity trading and FX trading is the longevity of the trend. Equity traders look for trends lasting weeks or months. Their focus is on well-defined trend breakouts or well-defined trends entered at points of temporary weakness.

With FX trading, the time frame — time in the market — is reduced. The leverage component means good profits are generated from moves equity traders would generally ignore. The search for FX opportunity starts with the 5-ADR range of price for each of the currency pairs. Figure 23.2 shows how GMMA analysis and the 5-ADR calculations come together.

The GMMA analysis confirms a bullish trend for GBPCAD. An entry around 1.9228 has a profit target near 1.9359 and the potential to go higher. This is a rebound and continuation of longer-term uptrend

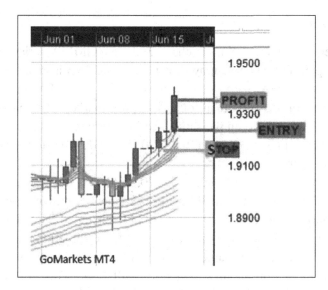

**Figure 23.2.** FX trade time frame.

breakout. Price is clustered in the upper section of the short-term GMMA. The initial stop is just below the upper section of the short-term GMMA.

The objective is to trade a portion of the next day's price movement with an 85% probability of a 131-pip move in the GBPCAD pair.

Here is the key difference. For equity traders, this 1-day rally rebound is assessed as part of a longer-term trend continuation. For our FX trading approach, this 1-day rally rebound is the entire trade. We want to capture the 131-pip move and then close the trade because we do not have the resources to actively monitor the continuation of this trend in a 24-hour global market.

The same trend and trend change relationships used on the Daily chart are applied to the 5 minute, 10 minute, 30 minute, or hourly chart where each candle represents a different time period. It's no longer useful to talk of long-term investors and short-term traders, but the same trend and trend change relationships remain. What makes the GMMA indicator so powerful is its fractural repetition, allowing it to be used over multiple time frames.

## Super Guppy

A number of previous FX trade charts include a GMMA variation with a Super Guppy. The Super Guppy shown in Figure 23.3 is an adaptation of the original GMMA, modified to work better in frothy FX markets with higher levels of volatility than found in equity markets. The primary difference is no gap between the short- and long-term groups of averages.

The Fast Guppy is 30, 35, 40, 45, 50, 55, and 60 period exponential moving averages.

The Super Guppy is 75, 90, 105, 120, 135, 150, 165, 180, 195, 210, 225, 240, 255, 270, 285, and 300 period exponential moving averages.

The analysis concepts are the same: a well-separated Super Guppy and a well-separated Fast Guppy indicate good trend direction and strength. When the Super Guppy bulges and develops very wide separation then there is a higher probability of a price pull back. This enables better identification of unsustainable price bubbles. This also delivers "fade-the-trend" opportunities where a trade is taken counter to the direction of the

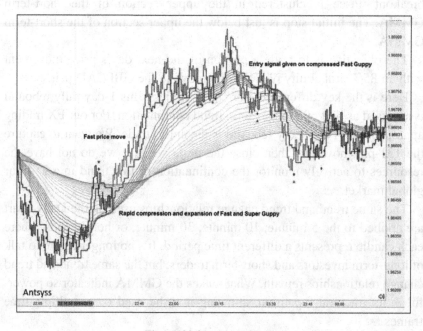

**Figure 23.3.**   Super Guppy.

rally when rapid compression in the Fast Guppy confirms a bubble collapse. These bubble opportunities are a feature of FX markets.

Despite the disparity in the length of averages, compression and crossover may develop very quickly in the Fast and Super Guppy. The Super Guppy helps anticipate fast moves in a volatile market and is best applied in smaller time frames such as 10 and 30 minutes.

The strategic GMMA trend analysis applied to a Daily chart is designed to identify the best trading candidate in the five currency pairs with the highest 5-ADR range. Trades are then protected with a method designed to protect capital and open profits as the trade moves towards the target level. We use a newly empowered old friend from equity markets.

## Creating GMMA in MT4

Creating the GMMA in MT4 takes just a few minutes to set as a template. Open a chart then go to Navigator on the left-hand side of the MT4 platform. Alternatively, press "Ctrl + N".

When the Navigator is open, expand the Indicator list and then expand the "Trend" sub-list. Locate the "Moving Average" option. Click and drag the moving average onto the chart. Open the moving average dialogue box to set the parameters of the moving average. Add the 12 exponential moving averages required for the GMMA. Right click on the chart and select "template" and then "save template" with a new name.

Whenever you want to apply the GMMA to an MT4 chart, right click on the chart, go down to "templates", and select GMMA template from the list. This can also be set as a default display template so every time you open a chart it includes the GMMA.

# Chapter 24

# FX Protection

Old friends are valued for their reliability, and even more so if they can adapt to new circumstances. Taken straight from our box of equity trading skills, we apply the Traders ATR in FX markets to manage stops and protect profits. The concept of ATR was developed by the brilliant technical analyst Welles Wilder. It captures the average volatility of price movements so we know which price movements are around average and which are larger than average. We call our adaptation of this long-term tool in our traders toolbox the Traders ATR because our application and display of the indicator is different.

We want answers to the most pressing questions in an FX trade: How to set a tight stop, so risk is reduced when the trade is first entered and how to manage the developing trade with an accurate trailing Stop Loss to protect profits? The Traders ATR provides an answer uniquely suited to FX short-term trades.

Unfortunately, at this point, we must wade into an alphabet soup. The focus of this chapter is on the Traders ATR. This is not to be confused with the 5-day ADR discussed in Chapter 23. These indicators measure different aspects of price behaviour. The 5-day ADR is used to select and build a trading pool. The Traders ATR is used to manage a trade.

Readers interested in the construction of the Welles Wilders ATR can flip to the note at the end of the chapter. Our particular interest is in the way the indicator is displayed on the screen and used, so this does not require a working knowledge of the ATR calculation. Suffice to understand, the ATR calculation captures the average expected range of price movement. Moves larger than average potentially signal an end to the current trend. This signal is used to exit the trade.

Traditionally, the ATR value is displayed below the price chart in a separate screen window. The value of the ATR increases and decreases as price volatility changes. For our purposes, the essential useful information is obscured in this unrestrained movement. The first modification step introduces a rachet mechanism so only movements in one direction are recorded. When the ATR value drops in a long-side trade, the previous higher ATR value is retained. These values are displayed as a line and moved to the main price display. The result is a line placed under a rising trend or above a falling trend. Figure 24.1 summarises the issues. The use of the ratchet and the ATR display directly on the price chart makes this a Traders ATR.

Some traders use this as a stand-alone method for trend and trend breakout trading but it's more common to use it alongside other indicators as shown in many of the previous examples. *Guppy Trading* includes more exacting details of the Traders ATR.

Our FX interest is only in the way it is used as a Stop Loss and protect profit feature. The trend breakout or strength is established with the 5-day ADR and GMMA analysis.

Traders ATR is available on the MT4/5 platform. Download at https://www.mql5.com/en/market/product/29683. It is also available in the

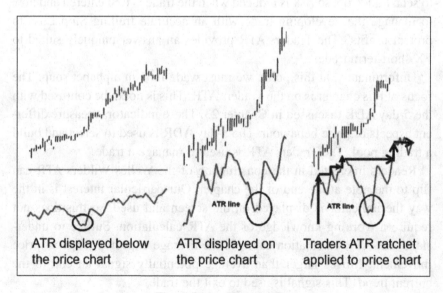

ATR displayed below the price chart

ATR displayed on the price chart

ATR line

Traders ATR ratchet applied to price chart

ATR line

**Figure 24.1.**   Traders ATR.

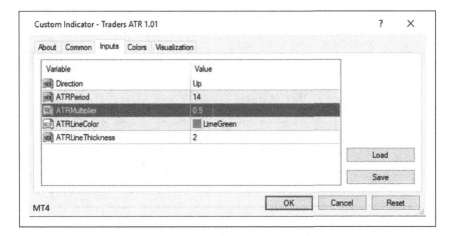

**Figure 24.2.** MT4 ATR.

Guppy Indicator toolbox with Metastock. The application of the indicator is very simple and easy to use. A simple click and drag from the MT4 indicator list puts the indicator onto the chart and then complete the dialogue box, as shown in Figure 24.2. The user then specifies the starting point for the calculation.

Here, we use the default 14-period ATR calculation, but change the ATR multiplier from the default 2×ATR to 0.5×ATR. These values are all fully customisable to suit your time frame or trading style. On the 4-hour charts, a tight 0.5×ATR facilitates earlier trade entry.

In FX trading, the Traders ATR is applied to an intraday chart and used to manage the trade as price moves towards the 5-day ADR target.

The Traders ATR is combined with a GMMA. We read the GMMA to determine trend direction. In this example, Figure 24.3, we anticipate a down trend. The GMMA confirms a trend change so when price breaks below the long-term Super Guppy, we enter short with confidence.

There are two ways to exit the trade, and this sits at the core of the ANTS-lite FX trading method. The first sets a static profit level using the 5-day ADR calculation. This target is achieved in this trade.

The second uses the Traders ATR as a trailing profit Stop Loss, closing the trade when price moves beyond the Traders ATR. This allows the trade to develop beyond the 5-day ADR target price.

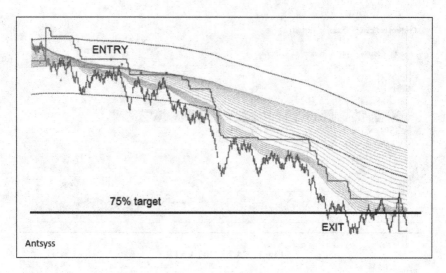

**Figure 24.3.** Traders ATR as a Stop Loss.

The movement from entry towards the target is managed with the Traders ATR acting as a trailing Stop Loss. This triggers an earlier exit if the trade development fails to reach the 5-day ADR target level.

Don't have ATR on your charting programme? A good news alternative comes from another old friend, the Count Back Line first introduced in *Share Trading*. It's not quite as accurate as the Traders ATR, but when applied as a trailing protect profit stop on these short-term FX trades, it delivers a very respectable result. The Count Back Line used in an FX environment is only applied as a protect profit stop. Unlike its equity trading application, it is not used as an entry signal. On balance, we prefer the Traders ATR, but the Count Back Line is also effective as shown in Figure 24.4 where an exit signal is delivered after the target price was reached.

Success in the FX markets depends on further honing these trading methods because the higher level of leverage available rapidly makes any mistake a costly one. All the methods we have discussed so far are combined into the ANTS-Lite approach. It's a robust, reliable approach to identifying and trading short-term FX opportunities. We hone this method further by adjusting the way price movement is displayed and analysed.

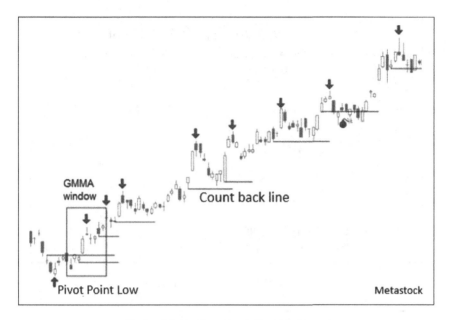

**Figure 24.4.** Count back line Stop Loss.

This explains why some earlier trade charts included the label 3R or 5R. For many readers, the robust ANTS-Lite solution is more than adequate. Others want to hone this further with an understanding there is no way to avoid the inevitable complexity. Read on if this is for you, but if not, then skip Chapter 25 and go to Chapter 29.

## ATR Construction

The ATR concept was developed by Welles Wilder to define the true range activity of price. Once calculated, this is used to understand the volatility of price. Moves above or below the ATR value — exceptional volatility — are often associated with a change in the trend. Figure 24.5 shows how the ATR is calculated.

130 is the value for the ATR for 1 day. If we are calculating a 5-day ATR then the value is calculated for each of the previous four days, as shown in Figure 24.6.

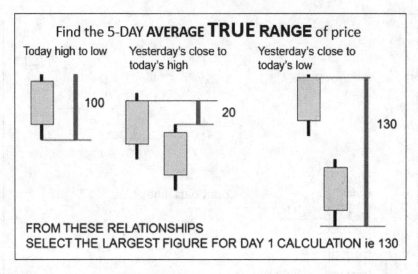

**Figure 24.5.** Calculating the ATR.

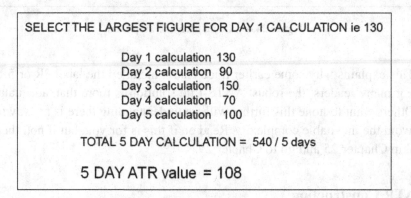

**Figure 24.6.** 5-day ATR value.

This value shows the expected price volatility on average over the 5-day period. It's a very useful figure for determining when a price move is larger than the average price volatility. This value is used to manage a stop and define trends.

# Chapter 25

# Home on the Range

What's more important: price or time? Ask the floor traders from the old open outcry trading pits and they will tell you price is more important than time, so they recorded trading activity with a point and figure chart, noting X and O for up and down price movements. Equity trades prefer price and time, so standard market charts have one candle displayed for each selected time segment and a time scale at the bottom of the chart.

In Chapter 21, we discussed the problem of selecting the correct time frame for a 24-hour market with multiple trading sessions. Ultimately it didn't worry us because we are trading on a single session basis, so the 5-minute price chart always looks the same no matter which market region we trade.

When applying strategic GMMA analysis to the top five candidates selected based on the 5-day ADR, the Daily chart, usually based on the New York open, is pretty good. But, and it's a significant but, analysis is improved if we drop the time element and focus purely on the price activity.

This allows the trader to focus only on the price move and, surprisingly, it improves the accuracy of the GMMA signals and the sensitivity of the Traders ATR as a means of managing an open trade. Using price range as a filter on the chart display significantly increases the reliability of trading signals. There are four things to notice on the range bar chart display in Figure 25.1.

**Figure 25.1.** ATR and range bar charts.

1. The display uses bars rather than candles.
2. The time frame scale is erratic. During periods of no price movement, the time frame is compressed. During periods of high activity, the time frame is expanded to show the price movement.
3. The construction of the range bar captures significant movements. The shift to a new bar is determined by price activity, not by time elapsed. This is the same as a point and figure chart and allows the trader to drill down on periods of significance.
4. The ATR stop is applied not to price, but to changes in the activity of price based on range breakouts. The ATR becomes a derivative of a derivative and this significantly improves reliability.

Some readers are satisfied with just the conclusion, but explaining how we get there is important because it provides a higher level of confidence in this unfamiliar range bar chart display. It also explains the meaning of the 3R and 5R notations on some of the earlier charts. It's a long and complicated story, so bear with us as we guide you through the process. Be warned, this is a philosophical diversion down one of the neglected byways of analysis and not for the faint-hearted.

Originally developed in Japan, candle stick charts are just one part of a Japanese solution to understanding price activity. Recording the open, high, low, and close in a defined time period is easy. Deciding which price movements are important and which are insignificant is a different challenge. The Japanese came up with several solutions — Kagi, 3-line break, and Renko charting. In the West, the solution to the same problem emerged as point and figure charting.

I cut my trading teeth with point and figure because it provided a unique solution to the paucity of time information I had when I was trading in the Australian outback with only one newspaper a week for reference. It revealed the skeleton of the market. Later I worked with Thomas Dorsey and Jeremy Du Plessis. They are the leading proponents of point and figure charting. Point and figure charting is discussed in more detail in *Share Trading*. Without access to daily price information or news, it made sense for me to focus on price action. Now the same concept is applied to the FX market, not because of the dearth of news, but because of the flood of news.

In FX markets there are often extended periods of mind-numbing boredom with little price movement. We want to eliminate the background noise and focus just on the high probability points where price activity offers better opportunity. The choice of the display feature on the chart assists in this task. To understand why we start at the beginning with a quick refresh of the problem, it's so that readers can have confidence the solution provides an appropriate answer.

The 24-hour nature of the market means the shape of the candle on the Daily charts depends on the market open you select — New York, London, or Asia. The core of the problem is shown in Figure 25.2, reprinted as a ready reference point.

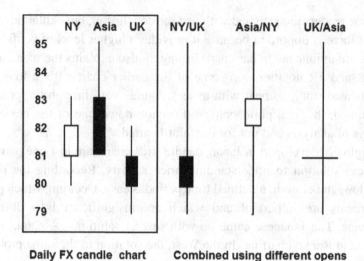

**Figure 25.2.** FX candle options.

Each candle has a different meaning depending on the starting point for the calculation. In one time frame we see a bearish candle, but in another time frame we see a bullish candle. Which candle is correct? This has a massive impact on the application of technical analysis to daily FX charts.

The solution is provided with a range bar chart which is a derivative of price. Range bars were developed by a Brazilian trader, Vicente Nicolellis. This price display is available in eSignal and with MT5. Like point and figure charts, range bar charts focus only on price, and to understand how they work, we compare these solutions with a "normal" time and price chart.

Chart A in Figure 25.3 shows two types of action defined by the vertical lines. Period 1 has a prolonged sideways movement where nothing really important happens. Then there is a fast breakout in Period 2. We really don't need to know much about the sideways movement in price. It just consumes chart space. However, we prefer to know a great more detail about the activity during the breakout.

The solution is to remove time from the equation and concentrate on the significant price movements. This is not a new concept. The point and figure chart is designed to do just this, but it is often a blunt tool as shown in Chart B.

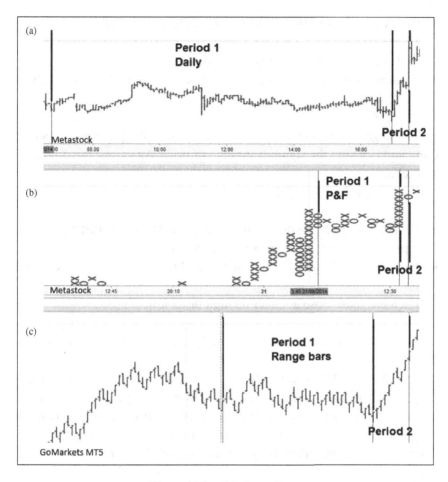

**Figure 25.3.** Display options.

The point and figure chart does a good job of compressing the sideways movement in price, but does a less successful job of providing more detail for the fast-moving breakout. The vertical lines show the same start dates as on the daily time-based chart.

Time is removed from the point and figure display by setting a box and reversal size. All price moves less than 5 pips are ignored. When a 6-pip move develops, a new X or O is added to the chart. X shows the up moves, and O shows the down moves. A modified attenuated time scale is directly related to the volatility and frequency of price movements.

The two features of the point and figure chart are as follows:

1. Sideways price activity is very compressed.
2. Fast up moves are also relatively compressed so analysis and trading is difficult.

The range bar display in chart C works on a similar principle of identifying and isolating the significant range of price. Again, we use 5 pips or a 5R chart.

Range bar rules are as follows:

- Each bar must have a high to low range equal to a specified number of pips, in this example 5 pips so it's a 5R chart.
- Each bar must open outside of the high/low range of the previous bar.
- Each bar must close at either its high or its low.

These rules make the range bar more dynamic than the point and figure chart.

Note the key differences between the point and figure chart and the range bar chart. The vertical lines show the same time period on all charts.

The sideways action is a little more extended than the same action on the point and figure chart. The breakout action contains considerably more trading details than either the point and figure chart or the daily price chart.

- Time is removed from the display.
- Sideways movement is less compressed than point and figure chart.
- The fast up move shows more price activity detail than the point and figure and daily bar chart, so analysis and trading is more effective.

Range bars bring significant advantages to the analysis of FX markets. Range bar charts can have any number of bars during a trading session. If there is high volatility, then there are more bars on the chart. If there is low volatility, then there are less bars on the chart.

Range bar charts smooth out price activity, removing insignificant price activity. They compress time, but not to the same extent as the point and figure chart. This leads to more accurate trend lines with more reliable trend line breaks. This is acknowledged as the primary advantage of range bar charts, although we do not apply this with short-term FX charts.

The range bar charts sharpen the ANTS trading approach and add a noticeable edge to the reliability of trading signals and management. The accuracy of trend break signals is improved when a GMMA indicator is applied to a range bar chart. An ATR protect profit stop applied to a range bar chart has fewer false exit signals. The accuracy of the stop is improved noticeably. The range bar chart also provides a solution to continuous daily charting of the FX market. The solution is summarised in Figure 25.4.

Perhaps some readers consider this a lengthy quibble about something relatively unimportant. We, and our trading results, beg to differ. The change in philosophical understanding — price is the most important element — enhances the accuracy of the two indicators we use for FX trading — the GMMA and the Traders ATR. It means a handful of trades are more successful and that's always a welcome addition to portfolio results. But rest assured, the robust ANTS Lite approach using the familiar price and time candle charts also delivers consistent and satisfactory results.

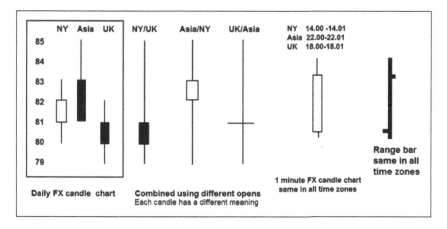

**Figure 25.4.** FX calculation options.

## Setting the Range

FX, Commodity, and Index markets are not the same and required different range bar settings to achieve the best analysis results. One size does not fit all. Our suggested preferences for these markets are shown in Figure 25.5.

| FX | Futures |
|---|---|
| **JPY pairs   1 pip = 0.001** | DOW Emini   1 tick = 1 |
| **Direction : 0.01 pip = 10R** | YM Direction : 10 tick = 10R |
| **Entry : 0.002 pip = 2R** | YM Entry : 2 tick = 2R |
| | NASDAQ/S&P Emini  1 tick = 0.25 |
| | NQ/ES Direction : 10 tick = 2.5R |
| | NQ/ES Entry : 2 tick = 0.5R |
| **All other FX pairs  1 pip = 0.0001** | Light Crude 1 tick = 0.01 |
| **Direction : 0.001 pip = 10R** | CL Direction : 10 tick = 0.1R |
| **Entry : 0.0003 pip = 3R** | CL Entry : 5 tick = 0.05R |
| | Gold 1 tick = 0.1 |
| | GC Direction : 10 tick = 1R |
| | GC Entry : 5 tick = 0.5R |

**Figure 25.5.**   Pip values.

# Chapter 26

# Scurry with the Ants

The beginning of a good equity trade has many different characteristics. It may move rapidly towards the target level as soon as the trade is entered. This is rare. Most often the trade moves slowly upwards. Occasionally the trade does nothing for a few days before starting to move up.

Lazy or superfast — it doesn't really matter in an equity trade because traders expect development to take days or weeks. This time risk is factored into the trade and management and is often just a glance at the closing price each day. Getting the entry exactly right is desirable but not essential.

Not so with FX markets. Time is a major risk factor because we don't want to carry the trade overnight. Entry as near as possible to the desired exact entry point is also essential because the impact of leverage is greater. Small mistakes grow rapidly, so the FX market is unforgiving. FX trading success depends on better analysis and entry accuracy than we are accustomed to in equity markets.

These demands are reflected in the core elements of the ANTS-Lite trading method we developed so we could transfer equity trading skills to the FX market. It combines market relationships, analysis, indicators, and a high probability outcome.

- The 5-day ADR identifies opportunities with the greatest probability of success.
- An enduring statistical relationship offers defined high probability rewards — an 85% probability of reaching 75% of the 5-day ADR value.
- A reliable and accurate method of setting expected exit targets.

- GMMA analysis confirms the probability of trend change or continuation and trend direction so traders know to go long or short.
- The Traders ATR stop is applied to the selected time frame — 3, 5, 10 minutes — to manage the trade as it moves towards the defined target level.
- The method is honed further with an advanced range bar chart display capturing significant price movement rather than time.

We apply ANTS-Lite trading to FX and commodity markets and to E-minis on the DOW and S&P. The approach is most effective in deep and liquid markets. The depth of FX market liquidity offers unique advantages for independent traders. Accuracy of trade entry is important, but trade management and trade exit determine the success of the trade.

The Traders ATR is applied to either a standard candlestick display or to a range bar chart. The range bar chart shown in Figure 26.1 is a 3R chart for an active currency pair with five hours trade duration. On the range bar chart, the Traders ATR stop is applied, not to price, but to changes in the activity of price based on range breakouts. The Traders ATR becomes a derivative of a derivative and this significantly improves reliability.

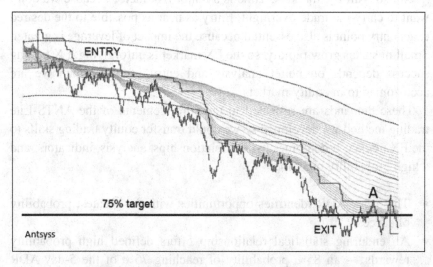

**Figure 26.1.** Classic FX trade using ADR and ATR.

At point A, price touches the value of the Traders ATR line. The exit signal is a close above the Traders ATR line and as this does not happen, the trade remains open and eventually reaches the target exit level. If this has been a standard 3-minute candle stick display using price and time then price would have closed above the Traders ATR line and triggered an early, and false, exit from the trend.

The trade target is 75% of the 5-day ADR and this value is plotted on the 3R or 5R chart. There is an 85% probability the 75% trade target will be achieved. Some traders continue to use the Traders ATR once the 75% target is hit and ride the trade further.

Our preference is to exit on a close below the 75% target level because this delivers consistent trading returns. In a very strong trend, the trade remains open. A very strong trend is defined by GMMA trend analysis discussed in other chapters. A close above the Traders ATR line before the 75% target is achieved is an exit signal.

There are three unique advantages with the ANTS method.

1. The identification of the underlying trend is improved when the GMMA is plotted using the closing price on a range bar chart. It allows for clearer trend definition.
2. When the Super Guppy component is calculated using the range bar, there is a clearer understanding of trend strength and trend limits. Bubbles are more easily identified and more reliably identify pull back and trend retracement opportunities using the Super Guppy.
3. The Traders ATR calculation uses the range bar price for the Stop Loss calculation. This delivers a more reliable ATR signal because price range is at the heart of the Traders ATR calculation.

Trading is a psychological game we play against ourselves. We give ourselves the best chance of winning by stepping back from the noise of the market so we make a more rational trading decision. We want to capture the pips from opportunities with the lowest risk profile. The ANTS-Lite method maximises our equity trading skills applied in different market conditions. In equity markets, we run with the bulls and hunt with the bears. In FX and commodity markets, we scurry with the ANTS.

# Chapter 27

# Best Time to Forex

Google finds endless search results of the best time to do many things. There are the best times to travel, fish, and even post on Facebook. Is there a "best" time to trade in the Forex market? There are times of the day where it seems to be no man's land, when spreads are wide and volumes are low, while at other times activity picks up and prices really start to move.

Additionally, economic news events move the Forex market, creating a volatile environment where the price of a currency pair may move sharply in seconds as a reaction to a particular news announcement. I avoid having an open trade around these news announcements and prefer alternative time periods of high-level price activity.

Approximately 30% of all Forex trades are made during the London session. Price volatility also increases when the US market opens, overlapping the trading session on the already open London market. When two markets overlap there is an increase in activity. The price range is larger than when only one market is open.

If you are trading in the Australian time zone, the following tables are a useful guide for market openings and market overlaps. Remember to take into account British Daylight Saving and New York Daylight Saving times where appropriate.

Pip movement during the Sydney/Tokyo market overlap is small as price tends to trade within a tight support and resistance range. There is more volatility in the hour of the Tokyo/Frankfurt overlap from the time the Frankfurt market has just opened and leading up to the London market open. Price activity often begins to pick up. Volatility increases sharply as soon as the London market opens. The Frankfurt/London overlap is a busy

**Table 27.1.** Market opening times.

| Forex Market | Session | |
| --- | --- | --- |
| | Australian Eastern Standard Time | Australian Eastern Daylight Time |
| Sydney | 7:00am–4:00pm | 7:00am–4:00pm |
| Tokyo | 10:00am–7:00pm | 11:00am–8:00pm |
| Frankfurt | 3:00pm–11:00am | 5:00pm–1:00am |
| London | 5:00pm–1:00am | 7:00pm–3:00am |
| New York | 10:00pm–7:00am | 12:00am–9:00am |

session, providing many opportunities for capturing larger pip movements. In terms of liquidity and highest activity, the best session for trading is later during the London/New York market overlap as highlighted in Table 27.1. More than 70% of my trades are made during this overlap period.

Here's an example of how we take advantage of these overlap periods. The following ANTSSYS trade was opened just before the open of the London Forex market as price activity begins to build momentum.

For this trade, I use the 7R chart for the general trend direction and a 3R chart for the entry chart. On the 7R long-term directional chart, the overall downward trend is well-defined. The short-term GMMA lines have compressed and turned down at the top of the chart and the long-term GMMA lines have also turned over, expanding in the downward direction. This confirms a short trade is suitable.

On the 3R short-term entry chart, both the short-term GMMA and long-term GMMA confirm the downtrend on the 7R charts. The lines of the short-term GMMA are showing signs of compression. This signals an upcoming price change either up or down. The 7R chart confirms a high probability of downtrend continuation.

A short trade on EURAUD is entered at 1.4129 with a Stop Loss at 1.4155 and a Take Profit target at 1.4099 for 30 pips. This is a straightforward trade, assisted by increasing liquidity and activity leading up to the London Forex market open. Price moved down, triggering an exit at the target of 1.4099 for a total of 30 pips.

If this trade had been placed earlier in the day during the Asian market session, the liquidity and activity is considerably less. From Table 27.1, this is when the Tokyo markets are open. Looking for a trade during the Asian session on the EURAUD 3R chart, Figure 27.1, shows price moving sideways within a band between 1.4155 and 1.4135 with a range of 20 pips. Movements are usually slower and smaller compared to the larger price movements made in the European and US sessions. Patience and realistic expectations of price movements are required when trading in the Asian session.

Ask me to choose the best time of day to trade the Forex markets and the answer is during the London/New York market overlap.

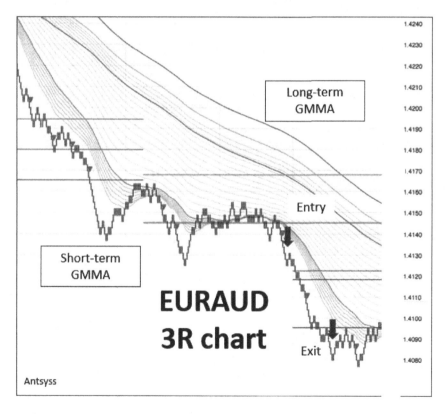

**Figure 27.1.** EURAUD 3R chart.

Unfortunately for those in the Australian time zone, it's also the best time of day to sleep.

Besides determining the best time to trade the Forex markets, there is also the consideration of how many pips are enough to capture in a trade. Surprisingly the answer is not always the more pips the better.

# Chapter 28

# Pip Fiction

Traders often translate a higher number of pips for higher profits. This is not always the case. Recently I attended a webinar where an attendee's reaction to the demonstrated trade was "... but that's only 38 pips". A trade with a high probability of capturing 38 pips is better than a 250-pip trade if the probability of price reaching this larger target is low.

Knowing the price per pip is essential so your position size is adjusted to your preferred capital risk amount. A high probability, lower pip trade, is not the choice for gamblers, so it should be your choice because trading is not gambling. Trading is the accurate management of risk. The following ANTSSYS trade illustrates the sound trading potential of "only 38 pips". It's a base example for further analysis of exit alternatives.

For this trade I use an 8R chart for the long-term time frame and a 3R chart for my entry.

On the 8R chart, Figure 28.1, the short-term GMMA have compressed and are gradually expanding before the entry point marked by the down arrow. Further downside movement is anticipated. The long-term GMMA lines are well separated, showing a strong downtrend in place.

On the 3R chart, Figure 28.2, the trend is also down.

A short trade is opened and entered at 1.3047 with a profit target of 1.2943 and a Stop Loss set at 1.3100. As the trade moves into profit, an ATR trailing Stop Loss on the directional 8R is employed to manage the trade to protect profit. At its best point on the chart, the trade was 77 pips in open profit. The ATR trailing Stop Loss was triggered and the trade was closed at 1.3009 for a profit of 38 pips.

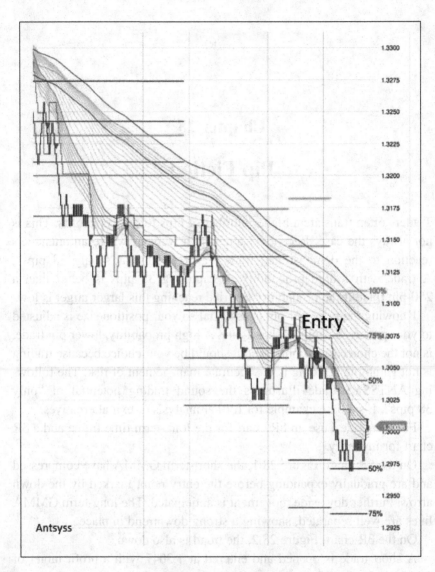

**Figure 28.1.** GBPUSD 8R chart.

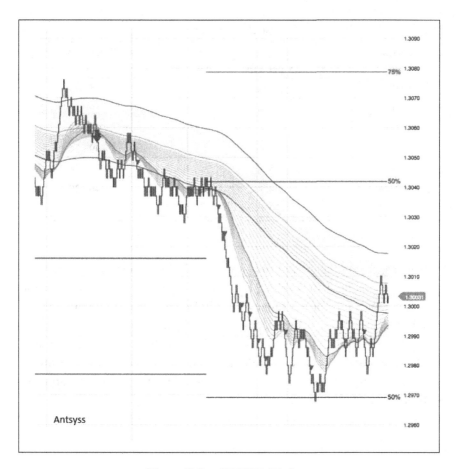

**Figure 28.2.** GBPUSD 3R chart.

Only 38 pips? Should we be satisfied? Table 28.1 compares different position sizing and how it affects profitability based on a Take Profit size of 38 pips.

The profit amounts change depending on the calculated unit size. Based on a risk/reward ratio of 1:1, the take-profit amounts are also potential loss amounts from your trading capital.

So, next time think about what 38 pips has the potential to be. It could be $49.40 but it could also be $4932.02. Knowing the price per pip is key.

*Stocks and Forex Trading*

**Table 28.1.** GBPUSD.

| Position Size Units | $ per Pip | No of Pips | Take Profit $ |
|---|---|---|---|
| 10,000 | 1.30 | 38 | 49.40 |
| 20,000 | 2.60 | 38 | 98.80 |
| 50,000 | 6.49 | 38 | 246.62 |
| 100,000 | 12.98 | 38 | 493.24 |
| 200,000 | 25.96 | 38 | 986.48 |
| 500,000 | 64.90 | 38 | 2466.20 |
| 1,000,000 | 129.79 | 38 | 4932.02 |

When calculating the capital risk amount, adjust the position size accordingly. The potential in a high probability, lower pip trade will become obvious. Don't fall for the fallacy of "pip fiction". It's more than just the number. Position size is the hidden gem in FX trading.

Maximising profit is a goal for every trader. Each time a decision is made on a trade as to when to take a profit, we can never know if this is the perfect time to take it. Alternative strategies are required in order to optimise our profit taking.

# Chapter 29

# Larger Piece of the Pie

We all want to increase our profitability in the market. The question is how to get a bigger piece of pie given the different choices of strategy, money and risk management, and other factors available to us. There are times when FX markets are unable to give you your full slice. More often than not it's because price fails to reach the Target Profit.

Successful trading rests on rigorous trade post-mortems to understand the reasons for success and for failure. By analysing this recurring failure to reach the target, I found ways my trades could be managed to maximise profits. This is the way I complete this analysis.

Table 29.1 shows 10 trades where I took money out of the market. First, target and Target Profit prices are calculated based on the factors discussed in full in previous chapters. These are support and resistance levels, liquidity gaps, and big figure numbers seen on a 1-hour chart. Typically the Target Profit is 14 to 30 pips. For the purpose of these tables, it was not necessary to distinguish between long and short trades. For ease of comparison, the dollar per pip is set at $100 for all positions.

My strategy involved closing half of my position when price reaches a predetermined number of pips before reaching the actual Target Profit. The Stop Loss is then moved a few pips away from break-even. By closing half of the position, my dollar per pip is reduced from $100 to $50 per pip when profit is taken and this part of the trade is closed. The remaining position is also closed at $50 per pip as there is only half the number of units remaining in the trade.

It's a solid profitable strategy, but there are times when many trades partially closed at the first target do not reach the Target Profit so the remaining position closes around break-even. Is closing the whole trade at the first

**Table 29.1.** Actual trade results.

| FX Pair | Pip Value $ | Take Money @ First Target | Profit/ Loss $ | Pip Value $ | Remaining Position to Target or Stopped Out | Profit/ Loss $ | Total Profit/ Loss $ | Total Pips |
|---------|-------------|---------------------------|----------------|-------------|---------------------------------------------|----------------|----------------------|------------|
| EURUSD | 50 | 7 | 350 | 50 | 11.6 | 580 | 930 | 18.6 |
| AUDJPY | 50 | 9.1 | 455 | 50 | −3.5 | −175 | 280 | 5.6 |
| CADJPY | 50 | 6.9 | 345 | 50 | 12.7 | 635 | 980 | 19.6 |
| EURJPY | 50 | 5.7 | 285 | 50 | −0.1 | −5 | 280 | 5.6 |
| USDJPY | 50 | 6.2 | 310 | 50 | 0.1 | 5 | 315 | 6.3 |
| EURUSD | 50 | 8 | 400 | 50 | 0.1 | 5 | 405 | 8.1 |
| EURUSD | 50 | 6.3 | 315 | 50 | 0 | 0 | 315 | 6.3 |
| AUDJPY | 50 | 7 | 350 | 50 | 0.1 | 5 | 355 | 7.1 |
| USDJPY | 50 | 6.2 | 310 | 50 | 0.1 | 5 | 315 | 6.3 |
| EURJPY | 50 | 7.3 | 365 | 50 | 16 | 800 | 1165 | 23.3 |
| **TOTAL** | | | | | | | **5,340** | |

target better than letting the whole trade run? Table 29.2 shows the profitability of this alternative strategy on the 10 trades shown in Table 29.1.

The captured profits are a lot better. The overall difference was a 31% increase in profitability over the returns from the actual trades.

Let's explore the compromise and simulate what happens if we take 2/3 of the position out of the market at first target instead of only 1/2 of the position. Surely the result is a larger slice of the pie? Table 29.3 shows what happens if we close 2/3 of the position at the first target, moved the stop to close to break-even, and let the remaining position run.

Surprisingly, the total profit from closing 2/3 of the position for $67 per pip then the rest for $33 was not significantly higher than the actual trades in Table 29.1 where we closed 1/2 of the position first for $50 per pip. The total increase in return over the actual trades was only 10% compared with 31% when closing the entire trade at first target for $100 per pip.

Considering the 10 trades overall, closing the whole position at the first target was optimal in seven out of the 10 trades. Of course, other factors like risk/reward need to be reconsidered if the original trading plan is changed.

**Table 29.2.** Trade closed completely at first target price.

| FX Pair | Pip Value $ | Close Trade @ First Target | Profit/ Loss $ | Return Over/ Below Actual Trade |
|---|---|---|---|---|
| EURUSD | 100 | 7 | 700 | −25% |
| AUDJPY | 100 | 9.1 | 910 | 225% |
| CADJPY | 100 | 6.9 | 690 | −30% |
| EURJPY | 100 | 5.7 | 570 | 104% |
| USDJPY | 100 | 6.2 | 620 | 97% |
| EURUSD | 100 | 8 | 800 | 98% |
| EURUSD | 100 | 6.3 | 630 | 100% |
| AUDJPY | 100 | 7 | 700 | 97% |
| USDJPY | 100 | 6.2 | 620 | 97% |
| EURJPY | 100 | 7.3 | 730 | −37% |
| **TOTAL** | | | **6,970** | **31%** |

**Table 29.3.** Closed 2/3 of trade position at first target.

| FX Pair | Pip Value $ | Take Money @ First Target | Profit/ Loss $ | Pip Value $ | Remaining Position to Target or Stopped Out | Profit/ Loss $ | Total Profit/ Loss $ | Total Pips | Return Over/ Below Actual Trade |
|---|---|---|---|---|---|---|---|---|---|
| EURUSD | 67 | 7 | 469.00 | 33 | 11.6 | 382.80 | 851.80 | 18.6 | −8% |
| AUDJPY | 67 | 9.1 | 609.70 | 33 | −3.5 | −115.50 | 494.20 | 5.6 | 77% |
| CADJPY | 67 | 6.9 | 462.30 | 33 | 12.7 | 419.10 | 881.40 | 19.6 | −10% |
| EURJPY | 67 | 5.7 | 381.90 | 33 | −0.1 | −3.30 | 378.60 | 5.6 | 35% |
| USDJPY | 67 | 6.2 | 415.40 | 33 | 0.1 | 3.30 | 418.70 | 6.3 | 33% |
| EURUSD | 67 | 8 | 536.00 | 33 | 0.1 | 3.30 | 539.30 | 8.1 | 33% |
| EURUSD | 67 | 6.3 | 422.10 | 33 | 0 | 0.00 | 422.10 | 6.3 | 34% |
| AUDJPY | 67 | 7 | 469.00 | 33 | 0.1 | 3.30 | 472.30 | 7.1 | 33% |
| USDJPY | 67 | 6.2 | 415.40 | 33 | 0.1 | 3.30 | 418.70 | 6.3 | 33% |
| EURJPY | 67 | 7.3 | 489.10 | 33 | 14.6 | 481.80 | 970.90 | 23.3 | −17% |
| **TOTAL** | | | **4,669.90** | | | | **5,848.00** | | **10%** |

**Table 29.4.** Maximum profits from trade period 16:00–23:00 AEST.

| FX Pair | Direction | Entry Price | High/Low for the Time Period 16:00–23:00 AEST | No. of Pips | Pip Value $ | Profit/ Loss |
|---------|-----------|-------------|-----------------------------------------------|-------------|-------------|--------------|
| EURUSD | Short | 1.1643 | 1.1596 | 47 | 100 | 4700 |
| AUDJPY | Short | 81.92 | 81.75 | 17 | 100 | 1700 |
| CADJPY | Short | 84.32 | 84.15 | 17 | 100 | 1700 |
| EURJPY | Short | 129.93 | 129.86 | 7 | 100 | 700 |
| USDJPY | Long | 113.04 | 113.14 | 10 | 100 | 1000 |
| EURUSD | Short | 1.1727 | 1.1686 | 41 | 100 | 4100 |
| EURUSD | Long | 1.165 | 1.1658 | 8 | 100 | 800 |
| AUDJPY | Long | 82.14 | 82.24 | 10 | 100 | 1000 |
| USDJPY | Long | 112 | 112.5 | 15 | 100 | 1500 |
| EURJPY | Short | 129.98 | 129.25 | 73 | 100 | 7300 |
| | | | | | **TOTAL** | **$ 24,500** |

Sometimes the strategy of getting the larger piece of the pie is not as obvious nor as profitable as it seems at first glance.

It is also useful to benchmark your trading results against the maximum theoretical result available. This gives an objective measure of absolute success rather than a yardstick complicated by real-time decisions or indecision. But please remember it is a theoretical exercise.

Table 29.4 uses the same actual trades as a base and calculates the maximum profit the market offered for each trade. These are ideal trades where the maximum profit is captured. We stay in the trade without the emotion of fear or greed. This is trading in a crystal ball environment.

The total profits from the real trades was $5,340, Table 29.1. This compares poorly with the total profit in Table 29.4 of $24,500. A profit there for the taking if each trade was perfectly executed. This leaves a staggering $19,160 on the table as the difference between the two approaches!

It is worth our while to explore further how we might capture more of the potential profit.

**Table 29.5.** Trading without taking any profits during the trade.

| FX Pair | Direction | Entry Price | Target Price/ Stop Loss Triggered | No. of Pips | Pip Value $ | Profit/Loss |
|---|---|---|---|---|---|---|
| EURUSD | Short | 1.1643 | 1.1622 | 21 | 100 | 2,100.00 |
| AUDJPY | Short | 81.92 | 82.03 | −11 | 100 | −1,100.00 |
| CADJPY | Short | 84.32 | 84.14 | 18 | 100 | 1,800.00 |
| EURJPY | Short | 129.93 | 130.16 | −23 | 100 | −2,300.00 |
| USDJPY | Long | 113.04 | 112.95 | −9 | 100 | −900.00 |
| EURUSD | Short | 1.1727 | 1.1709 | 18 | 100 | 1,800.00 |
| EURUSD | Long | 1.1650 | 1.1632 | −18 | 100 | −1,800.00 |
| AUDJPY | Long | 82.14 | **82.14** | 0 | 100 | 0.00 |
| USDJPY | Long | 112 | 111.86 | −14 | 100 | −1,400.00 |
| EURJPY | Short | 129.98 | 129.83 | 15 | 100 | 1,500.00 |
| | | | | | **TOTAL** | **$ −300** |

The trades in Table 29.5 assume the trade remains open until either the Stop Loss is triggered or price reaches the Target Profit. Stop Losses remain as originally placed.

Using this method, the consequences of not taking profit along the way was a loss $300. Greed did not pay well for every trade in this table. Out of the 10 trades, 40% reached the Target Profit, 50% were stopped out before reaching the Target Profit. The AUDJPY trade was left in limbo as price neither triggered the Stop Loss nor hit the Target Profit.

So the question is how to leave some profit on the table without feeling like we have missed out on massive amounts of profit?

The solution lies in price action strategy. The following intraday USDJPY trade uses a price action strategy to identify an opportunity to take money out of the market. This personal trade example brings together the strategies and approaches we have discussed in previous chapters and the lessons from the trade post-mortems.

Starting with the Daily chart, Figure 29.1, price is generally trending upwards. Price has more recently broken back up through the trendline for a possible resumption of the uptrend.

**Figure 29.1.**   USDJPY Daily chart.

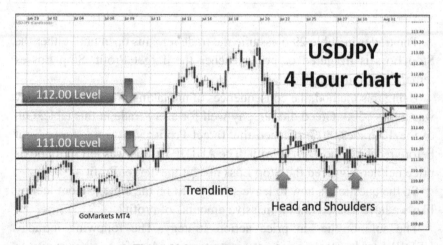

**Figure 29.2.**   USDJPY 4-hour chart.

On the 4-hour chart, a head and shoulders reversal pattern has formed under the main trendline as marked by the arrows. This is added confirmation of price wanting to turn and trend upwards again (Figure 29.2).

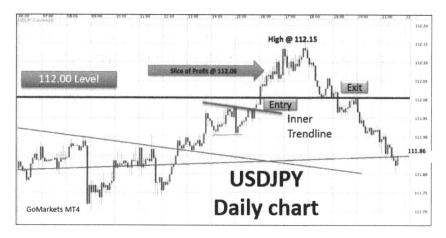

**Figure 29.3.** USDJPY 5-minute chart.

The trend direction on the longer timeframe charts of the Daily and 4-hour all agree that price is most likely going to continue in the upwards direction. The 5-minute chart is used to find an entry point.

Another inner trendline is drawn on the 5-minute chart (Figure 29.3). A break above and a back-end retest on this inner trendline triggers the conditions to open a long trade at 112. The Stop Loss is set at 111.86 and Take Profit is at 112.23. The first Profit Target is at 112.10. When price reaches 112.10, we close 2/3 of the position to take some profit out. Slippage meant the profit on this part of the trade was at 112.06 for $310. The Stop Loss is moved to breakeven at 112. Price reached a high of 112.15, formed a double top, then retraced towards the Stop Loss of 112. The trade closed at a very small profit of 0.1 of a pip when price triggered the Stop Loss at 112. The total profit made was $315.

Aiming for the largest piece of the pie might not always give you your desired outcome. The decision lies in whether you think receiving a thinner slice of the pie early is better than staying with a higher risk trade to get the largest piece and possibly missing out and ending up hungry. Sometimes it is preferable to take some profit out before price reaches the Target Profit. It is a better outcome than finding yourself in a losing trade as the end result.

The longer a trade is open, the longer the time period your capital is at risk. We want to find ways to be profitable and to capture as much of a trend as possible without getting entangled in a price spike against our trade or worse, a trend collapse.

# Chapter 30

# Time Matters as Trend Shatters

There is often a lot of media attention regarding the environment of volatility and uncertainty. Trend patterns do not seem to last as long or be as reliable as in the past. Consequently, time in the stock market has become a major risk factor. Many investment advisors persist in telling investors that time in the market is the most important component of success. Buy more as price falls, they suggest. Hold for the long-term and ignore the short-term price falls, they tell investors eager for reassurance.

Does this work? Sometimes it's successful, but most times it's a simple arithmetical relationship that works against you. The most disappointing rule of the market is that a 10% loss cannot be recovered with a 10% gain.

We look at three examples to explore these consequences. A good starting point to finding a good uptrend to trade is to enter into an existing established trend. Some trend traders like to find a stock making a new high because it's a sign it may continue to do so. This is not always a recipe for success, as the following three trade examples show. Time in the market does matter, but not in the way that many investment advisors suggest.

This is demonstrated in the Bapcor Limited (BAP) trade.

The BAP chart, Figure 30.1, is a perfect display of a well-established trend. Prices start from the left bottom corner flowing steadily upwards towards the upper right corner. This is a classic textbook example of an uptrend. The short-term GMMA has well-separated lines, and the long-term GMMA has evenly separated lines, indicating good support from long-term investors and a stable long-term trend.

The entry is at $5.30, Figure 30.2, with a targeted 10% return at $5.83 and a Stop Loss of $4.98 based on support levels identified on the

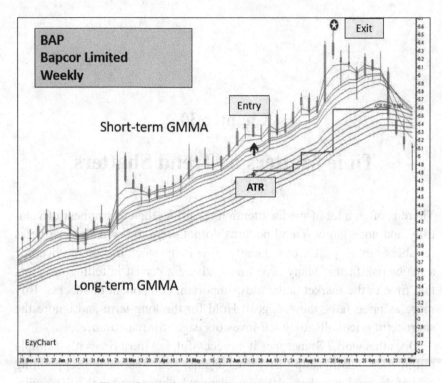

**Figure 30.1.** Bapcor Limited (BAP) Weekly chart.

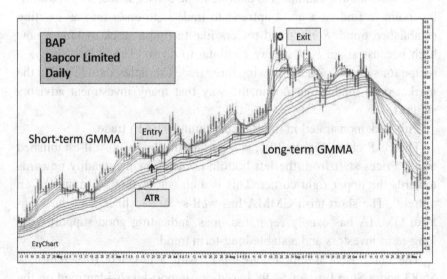

**Figure 30.2.** Bapcor Limited (BAP) Daily chart.

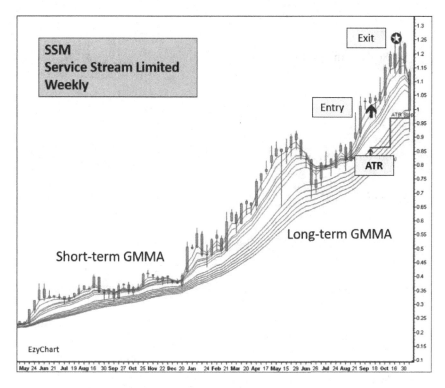

**Figure 30.3.**   Service Stream Limited (SSM) Weekly chart.

Weekly chart. In order to take advantage of the developing price momentum, the trade was not closed until a few days after the Target Profit was reached with an exit at $6.33. After this point, on the Daily and Weekly charts, price begins to fall. The short-term GMMA compresses, turns, and falls through the long-term GMMA. On the Daily chart, the short-term GMMA moved below the long-term GMMA in a definite downtrend. This former stable uptrend had collapsed.

The chart of SSM, Figure 30.3, looks like a good strong stock trending upwards. Separation of the moving average lines within the short-term GMMA and within the long-term GMMA shows strong support for this uptrend.

The entry is at $1.04 with a targeted 15% return of profit at $1.20 and a Stop Loss of $1.00 based on support and resistance levels. SSM reached its Target Profit price and the trade was closed at $1.20. After this point on

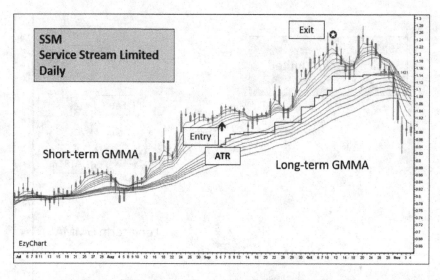

**Figure 30.4.** Service Stream Limited (SSM) Daily chart.

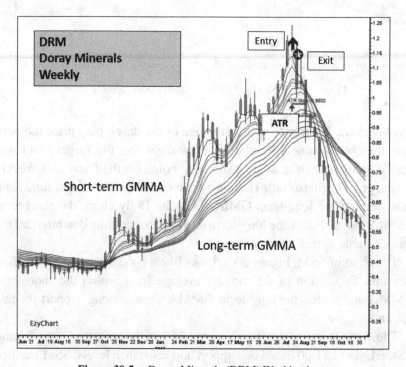

**Figure 30.5.** Doray Minerals (DRM) Weekly chart.

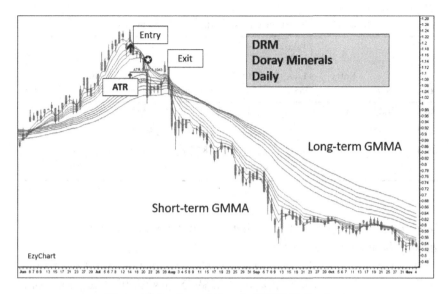

**Figure 30.6.** Doray Minerals (DRM) Daily chart.

the Daily chart, price retraces then tries to reach its previous high again (Figure 30.4). After making one more touch at this high, the short-term GMMA starts to turn and fall through the long-term GMMA. On the SSM Weekly chart, price plunges through the ATR Stop Loss. Another example of a stock with its trend foundations shaken.

Figure 30.5's chart also looks like a good established uptrend with strong support from investors, as shown on the long-term GMMA. It's also an example of what happens when you end up buying at the top of a trend.

Based on the DRM Daily chart, Figure 30.6, the entry for this trade is $1.22 with a Profit Target of $1.34 and a Stop Loss of $1.10. This trade had a very short life with the Stop Loss hit within days. As difficult as it was to accept the trade had not gone in the anticipated direction, the trade is closed as planned. The chart shows the consequences of not acting on the Stop Loss exit signal.

Table 30.1 summarises the outcomes from these trades. Alongside are the alternative outcomes from a buy and hold strategy favoured by

**Table 30.1.** Short-term trend trade versus buy hold strategy.

| Code | Units | Entry Price | Take Profit/ Loss Price | Profit/ Loss | % Return | Current Price | Buy Hold | % Return |
|------|-------|-------------|-------------------------|--------------|----------|---------------|----------|----------|
| DRM | 1000 | $1.22 | $1.10 | −$115.00 | −9.47% | $0.53 | −$685.00 | −56.38% |
| BAP | 1000 | $5.30 | $6.33 | $1,030.00 | 19.43% | $5.11 | −$190.00 | −3.58% |
| SSM | 2000 | $1.04 | $1.23 | $380.00 | 18.27% | $0.99 | −$100.00 | −4.81% |
| | | | | **$1,295.00** | | | −$975.00 | |

investment advisors who tell us that time in the market matters more than timing the market.

A basic timing of the market using a Take Profit or Stop Loss trigger delivers a $1,295 profit compared to a $975 loss for the "buy and hold" time in the market approach. Each of these stocks were making new highs as I sought to join the established trend. In the past, trends held their direction for longer. Today with the frequency of trend collapse, time in the market makes a difference to achieving good profits and limiting losses.

The methods for identifying and trading a trend apply to many financial instruments. In Chapter 31, we use technical analysis to assess the trend direction of the digital currency Bitcoin.

# Chapter 31

# Bitcoin Boom or Bust!

This is the attention-grabbing headline Boost Juice used for their four week competition to win one of four Bitcoins. "Guesstimate how much you think a Bitcoin's worth is going to be at 12pm the following Monday. The correct or closest guess WINS!" Sounds straightforward enough. Instead of just guessing, a closer look at the Bitcoin charts using simple technical analysis was considered a better foundation for my final answer and it also showed that these trading methods can be applied to unconventional financial market places.

Here's the detailed analysis, and it uses the same techniques we apply to the currency pairs considered in previous chapters. We didn't call the exact price, but this exercise shows that when it comes to trading, Bitcoin yields to the methods proven successful in trading other financial instruments.

On the Bitcoin Weekly chart, Figure 31.1, a steep rise in price culminates in the high of 19,891 on 17 December 2017. The EMAs of 10, 20, and 50 confirmed the uptrend. Despite price making a large retracement and bouncing off the trendline for a third time, the 10 and 20 EMAs turned down slightly but did not cross over. Starting from the bottom left-hand side of the chart, there is a low, a high, higher low, higher high, higher low, and a parabolic higher high followed by a higher low. The sloped trendline drawn has been hit in three places and is still intact. Technically the uptrend is still in place on the Weekly chart.

The Bitcoin Daily chart, Figure 31.2, shows a downward channel with price bouncing off the upper and lower boundaries. At the top of the chart, a head and shoulders pattern formed, presaging the downwards movement of price. The 10, 20, and 50 EMA lines turned over with the 50 EMA on

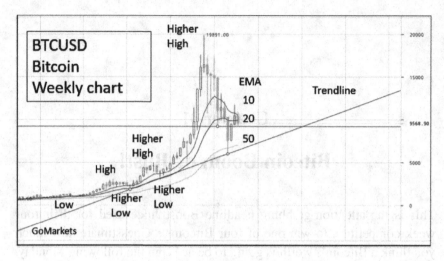

**Figure 31.1.**    BTCUSD Weekly chart.

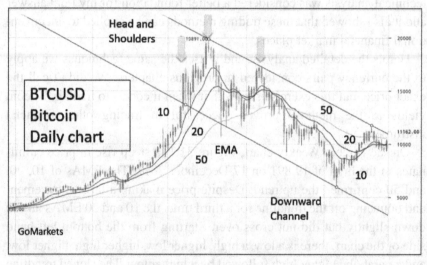

**Figure 31.2.**    BTCUSD Daily chart.

top. The trend is downwards, but if price breaks out of the top of the channel, we may see future rises in price.

In order to get closer to the shorter-term price action, we focus on analysing the 4-hour chart.

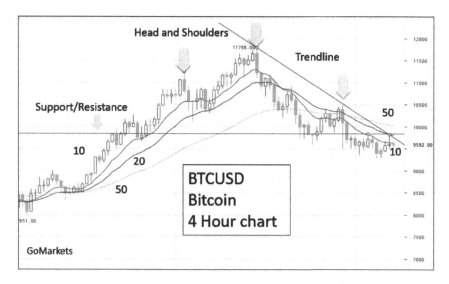

**Figure 31.3.** BTCUSD 4-hour chart.

The Bitcoin 4-hour chart, Figure 31.3, includes the formation of a head and shoulders pattern. Price broke the Support/Resistance line near 10,000. Two attempts to break above the Support/Resistance line were unsuccessful. Price retreated from the Support/Resistance line where its it intersected the downward trendline.

This chart analysis was made at the beginning of the week prior to the competition close. A couple of days before the closing day, I had another look at the 4-hour chart.

Figure 31.4 shows how price had broken through the trendline resistance and above the Support/Resistance line. At the same time the 10, 20, and 50 EMA confirmed a short-term uptrend with potential for price to reach the last high at 11,788. The head and shoulders pattern identified earlier for a downward movement in price had failed.

Using trendlines, Support/Resistance lines, and EMA lines together with a head and shoulders pattern enabled me to analyse the Bitcoin price for the competition. My "guesstimate" was based on the 4-hour chart.

Based on a 4-hour chart, the day before the close of week one of the competition, my target "guesstimate" was 11,530.47. When the

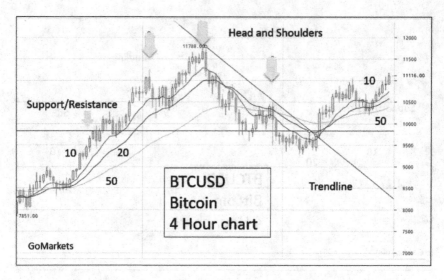

**Figure 31.4.** BTCUSD 4-hour chart development.

competition closed, the price of Bitcoin was at 11,594.88. The predicted target price based on technical analysis wasn't far off the actual price.

Technical analysis enables us to make sense of price movements and trend direction on the chart of Bitcoin by applying the same analysis methods we use for equities or FX. If the price of Bitcoin is heading for a boom or about to bust and drop, we see it coming through careful selection and application of technical analysis. Using technical indicators and patterns are a trader's advantage in all markets.

# About the Authors

**Karen Wong** is a private trader in equity and forex markets. She is a regular contributor to the "Tutorials in Applied Technical Analysis" newsletter published by Guppytraders.com and has published articles in "Your Trading Edge" and "Stocks and Commodities". Her passion for technical analysis grew from reading her very first trading book, *Share Trading* by Daryl Guppy. This inspired further study leading to a Graduate Certificate in Applied Finance and Investment and a Diploma in Technical Analysis. Wong is an internationally recognised Certified Financial Technician (CFTe) and Certified Practising Accountant (CPA). She enjoys learning from other traders and served in the Sydney Chapter Council of the Australian Technical Analysts Association for a couple of years before becoming President in 2020.

www.karenwong.net

**Daryl Guppy** has provided trading and investment analysis of financial markets for more than 25 years. He trades his own capital. He has a well-established public record of successful trade calls for trading global equity, commodity, and FX markets. He has unique experience in trading Western and mainland Chinese markets. Guppy has nine popular books published by John Wiley. These include *Trend Trading* and *The 36 Strategies of the*

*Chinese for Financial Traders*. Four of these books are available in Chinese.

He has developed several technical indicators which are included in industry standard software. Globally, many traders use the technical indicators developed by Guppy to trade equities and other markets.

Guppy provides strategic market analysis for CNBC business television and CGTN Global Business. He is a regular host anchor on CNBC Asia Squawkbox where he is known as "The Chartman". Guppy is a regular contributor for financial magazines and media in Singapore, Malaysia, China, Australia, and the US. He oversees the production of weekly analysis and trading newsletters.

He is in demand globally as a speaker at financial conferences and for the delivery of training for financial organisations particularly in Singapore, China, and other parts of Asia.

www.guppytraders.com

Printed in the United States
by Baker & Taylor Publisher Services